Something to Bear in Mind

A Heart-warming Pot-pourri of Yoga, Buddhism, Shamanism and Spiritual Philosophy
For Empowering Yourself

Something to Bear in Mind

A Heart-warming Pot-pourri of Yoga,
Buddhism, Shamanism and
Spiritual Philosophy
For Empowering Yourself

Michelle Corrigan

BOOKS

Winchester, UK
Washington, USA

First published by O-Books, 2012
O-Books is an imprint of John Hunt Publishing Ltd., Laurel House, Station Approach,
Alresford, Hants, SO24 9JH, UK
office1@o-books.net
www.o-books.com

For distributor details and how to order please visit the 'Ordering' section on our website.

Text copyright: Michelle Corrigan 2010

ISBN: 978 1 84694 819 0

A CIP catalogue record for this book is available from the British Library.

Design: Stuart Davies

Printed in the UK by CPI Antony Rowe
Printed in the USA by Offset Paperback Mfrs, Inc

We operate a distinctive and ethical publishing philosophy in all
areas of our business, from our global network of authors to
production and worldwide distribution.

CONTENTS

I would like to dedicate this book to all my family, teachers and friends.

About the Author

My Yoga journey began many moons ago in 1994 whilst on a two-year expatriate spell in Bangkok. I often visited the beautiful Thai Buddhist temples and went on a Meditation retreat run by Buddhist Monks which was in the form of Vipassana Meditation - Insight Meditation focusing on the breath and repeating Mantras (sacred sounds) on the rise and fall of the abdomen. Whilst in Bangkok, I also studied Thai massage - a wonderful body treatment whereby the energy lines are pressed with the thumbs and palms of the hands.

I then trained as an Aromatherapist in Dorking, England. I learnt a lovely body massage using bespoke aromatherapy oils and tracing meridians, making this a holistic treatment.

Whilst living in Devon, I trained as a Reiki Practitioner which introduced me to the esoteric body system. I also joined a meditation group which helped me with expanding the technique of visualization and opened up my spiritual awareness.

In 2002, I moved to Surrey with my family and set up my own meditation and healing groups and in 2004 I started my training with the British Wheel of Yoga as a Yoga Teacher.

I believe that once you are working with energies in ways such as Reiki, this 'opens up' the spiritual channels. Whilst doing a spiritual reading with my Teacher, I started to 'channel' which means that Spirits work through me to channel philosophy. This is to spread 'the word' to as many people as possible in order for a better balance to come back to them.

I realised that my path is to do deep Soul work and seek liberation so I have also spent time doing self-study and healing. I have spent some years looking at the Self, discovering who I am, my purpose for being here and healing at a soul level. I have found all the Tools mentioned in my book 'Your Quest for

Spiritual Knowledge - Preparing you for 2012 and Beyond' such as Shamanic Healing, Tarot, Crystals, Reiki and Numerology really life-changing.

Since 2005 I have been learning Shamanic practices with Leo Rutherford, Dawn Russell and Lorraine Grayston of Eagle's Wing College of Shamanic Medicine. I have attended workshops and courses for personal development and at Practitioner level including Trance Dance, Journeying and Soul Retrieval, The Medicine Wheel & Star Maidens Circle, Cauldron of Changes, Earth Child and Women Wild and Still – the rites of passage for women.

My Sanskrit name given to me by my great Yoga tutor - Swami Satchidananda Mataji, is "Mokshapriya" which means "She for who liberation is dear". In numerology, I am a number 5 which means I am here to do Soul work and work as a Master Healer and Spiritual Teacher, to pass on the higher truth.

My previous non-fiction books 'Your Quest for a Spiritual Life' and 'Your Quest for Spiritual Knowledge' are published by 'O' Books and I have recorded a Meditation CD 'Your Quest for Peace, Healing & Balance'. These are all available from Amazon.

Please visit my Website www.purplebuddha.co.uk

x

Introduction

'Something to bear in mind' is a heart-warming pot-pourri of Yoga, Buddhism, Shamanism and Spiritual Philosophy. Each day of the year, you will either be given a thought of the day which may be just that - a thought, or it may be an invitation to practice a meditation, connect with nature or a practical ceremony. You will visit your inner world and realize the Self, understand your make-up of the elements of earth, wind, fire, water and spirit. You will discover your place of healing and by doing so start to shift blocked energy and then connect to your Higher Self. You will also feel and see nature as the seasons change gaining a real connection with the beauty that Mother Earth provides us with. This will help to make you more rounded, more balanced so you can deal with what life throws at you. Stress is probably the highest cause of illness and relationship issues, and by being more balanced, you will learn to deal with life generally in a calmer way.

In brief, we go through life and seem to store blocked energy through traumas, experiences and in the process lose part of our life force. These techniques in this book will help you to live in the present, remove toxins, waste products, blocked energy from the body and help you to regain your life force which will make you feel more whole in mind, body and spirit. To live in peace and harmony is to live in beauty.

Introduction to Yoga

Yoga is union of the body, mind and spirit. This means knowing and understanding your mind and mastering it. Having body awareness and knowing your body's needs with regards to nourishment, nutrition and exercise. Spirit means connecting with your inner winds, your subtle body. The subtle body is the energy system within your physical body which includes energy centres known as the Chakras which are located up your spine and the three main channels are where these inner winds travel up and around the spine. One channel representing the Sun which is the Male and the other the Moon which is the Female. The middle channel holds a balance of the two energies and this energy when balanced travels up this channel and into the energy centre of the brow which is linked to the mind. When all is good in life and you have a regular daily spiritual practice, this energy will travel smoothly and you will feel balanced and enlightened. This energy is known as your kundalini energy which lays dormant in the base energy centre of your body and as you journey along on your spiritual path, the energy rises to your brow centre. In deep states of meditation you will then receive commands and guidance from The Divine or The Higher Self, through this centre. Wisdom and Intuition then develops. The mind becomes steady and strong and very in tune with the inner winds (energy). When things are not so good in life and you are out of balance, the inner winds get blocked and clog up your chakras. This can lead into illness of the body and the mind.

A Yogic state of mind would mean you are focused, enjoy just being, live in the present moment and are generally a balanced person to be around. Yoga is often thought of as a means of exercise but there is much more depth than just the physical aspect. There are eight limbs of Yoga which are the framework known as Ashtanga. These eight limbs include the codes of conduct and vows of life which are the spiritual laws, movement of the body in the form of stretching through the postures, breathing techniques, going inwards rather than living in an outer world, concentrating the mind, being fully focused and sustaining concentration in meditation, reaching liberation and freedom, also known as enlightenment.

The Eight Limbs of Yoga are as follows:

Yamas – Spiritual laws that affect the outer world such as non-violence, right speech, not stealing, moderation, non-greed.

Niyamas – Spiritual laws affecting the Self such as cleanliness of mind and body, being content, self-discipline, self-study, connecting to The Great Divine.

Asana – Yoga postures

Pranayama – Breathing techniques

Pratyahara – taking focus inward

Dharana – Concentration

Dhyana – Meditation

Samadhi – enlightenment, freedom from suffering, liberation

Regular practice of postures, breathing techniques and meditation will bring peace and harmony to the mind, body and spirit. Discipline is required as regular practice is needed but the benefits will be enormous.

To connect to the true Self releases you from your neurotic self – the fragmented you, suffering is released, brings you to your centre, so you can live with love and peace and find true freedom and liberation.

Introduction to Buddhism

Like Jesus, Buddha lived an earthly life – here as a person in a physical body. Buddha was earlier than Jesus by around 500 years. He found enlightenment through Meditation and contemplation by sitting under a Bodhi Tree in what is now Lumbini, Nepal. Enlightenment meaning freedom of suffering and reaching liberation. Once enlightened he met up with five Mendicants who he once was associated with. All five of them became enlightened and became his disciples and were ordained as monks. They went on to enlighten more and eventually there were 60 enlightened beings who became the order of monks that passed on his teachings.

The teachings are known as 'Dharma' and there are different movements of Buddhism, among them Theravada, Mahayana and Vajrayana. These teachings spread right across Asia and more recently into the West.

Buddhism is a path of practice and spiritual development leading to Insight into the true nature of life. Buddhist practices such as meditation are means of changing yourself in order to develop the qualities of awareness, kindness, compassion, love and wisdom. Buddhists continually practice being mindful, being present and living in the now. Buddhism suggests kindness, compassion and love essentially for the Self as well as for others. Wisdom is a gift that we all have deep inside and it is through Meditation, study of texts, self-development and 'peeling off the layers of baggage' and detaching the Self from desires and unhealthy attachments in life, that this gift can be discovered.

Techniques of meditation tend to be very simple, focusing on the breath for example, one technique being Vipassana Meditation which means Insight, and mindful meditation. Mindfulness is a type of meditation that essentially involves focusing on your mind in the now – in the present. To be mindful is to be aware of your thoughts and actions in the present, without judging yourself. While concentration involves the practitioner focusing their attention on a single object. The object being either a Mantra which is a sacred sound, word or several words or a visualization such as a Lotus flower or imagining yourself in a healing temple or sitting on top of a mountain for instance.

Because Buddhism does not include the idea of worshipping a creator God, some people do not see it as a religion in the normal, Western sense. The basics of Buddhist teaching are straight-forward and practical - nothing is fixed or permanent, actions have consequences (karma – plant the seeds and watch them grow in other words what energy you put out to the world, watch it come back to you), change is possible.

There are around 350 million Buddhists and a growing number of them are Westerners. They follow many different forms of Buddhism, but all traditions are characterised by non-violence, lack of dogma, tolerance of differences, and by the regular practice of meditation. Buddhists tend to describe the Soul as 'Consciousness' and they believe that we will have many lives (as do Hindus) and it is our mission to find liberation from suffering.

Being in a Buddhist Temple or in the presence of a statue of Buddha brings such beautiful peace. Simple Buddhist chants such as repeating sacred words such as 'Buddho' or 'Om Mani Padme Hum' help to focus the mind, connect to the inner Self and bring the beauty of peace and harmony to mind, body and spirit. Buddhism is very practical as you can practice anywhere rather than having to go to a place of worship.

Introduction to Shamanism
Shamanism is simply being connected to Earth energies, which means to nature, being grounded, feeling linked to Mother Earth, as well as being connected to The Great Divine, to Spirit energies. This means to walk in both worlds.

Shamanism is an anthropological term referencing a range of beliefs and practices regarding communication with the spiritual world. A practitioner of shamanism is known as a shaman (pronounced 'shayman' or 'shahman'.)

Shamanism embodies the belief that shamans are intermediaries or messengers between the human world and the spirit worlds. Shamans are said to treat ailments/illness by mending the soul. Alleviating traumas affecting the soul/spirit restores the physical body of the individual to balance and wholeness. The shaman also enters spiritual realms or dimensions to obtain solutions to problems afflicting the community. Shamans may visit other worlds/dimensions which means entering an altered state of consciousness by Journeying using the healing sound of the drum which is known as 'The Shaman's Horse' to bring guidance to misguided souls and to heal at a soul level. The shaman operates primarily within the spiritual world, which in turn affects the human world. The restoration of balance results in the elimination of blocked energy caused by trauma and illnesses.

Generations ago, every village would have had a Shaman or Medicine Man or Woman; someone who would have provided medicine from herbs and plants grown around them, someone who would have given healing to those who were in need, which means healing channeled from Spirit. Shamans would have provided divination to those who wanted insight. In Great Britain we have Pagans and Druids who also honour the same values as Shamans, which is nature-based spirituality and used medicine circles but perhaps were or were not called Shamans as such. The traditions have been kept going in certain cultures like the Siberians, Native American Indians, Mayans of South America and the Incas of Peru, despite attempts at repression by some. Their methods vary, but the essence of respecting Mother Earth and linking to Spirit remains the same for all. At the present time there are more and more Shamanic Practitioners being trained, which is perhaps what is needed. Shamanic Practitioners can reach the Soul in a more direct and effective way. This means the Client can be brought back into their own power, they can connect back to their centre. Blocked energy is removed from the body through healing techniques such as Soul Retrieval, and lost life force is returned. The Client can then go from being neurotic and fragmented, to whole and balanced. As humans, we form unhealthy attachments to past wounds and traumas and find it difficult to let go, move on and live life in love and joy.

Shamanic healing differs from other forms of healing such as Reiki, as the energy is different. If you have experienced Angel Healing or Reiki Healing, although the energy is beautiful and has its own value, it is much more subtle compared to that of Shamanic healing which seems to be much more direct, to the point, rather like drilling with a pneumatic drill - very powerful and effective!

It takes a real Warrior to take the path of self-development and healing.

Before You Begin

You are ready to embark on a New Year which can bring changes for the better if you wish. Why not write a journal of your spiritual journey, your healing path, not only is it therapeutic but it makes very interesting reading later on and shows you how you have developed and evolved.

Chapter One

1st January

A New Year begins which brings to you fresh energy! Leave the energy of last year behind you, begin your spiritual practice *now*. See this as a new door opening and old door closing.

How are you today – physically, mentally and emotionally? Physically – your body, mentally – your mind and emotionally – your feelings?

What changes can you bring in to your life? Perhaps some form of body movement – Yoga maybe? Keep your energy fresh by eating well, and follow a good balanced diet know your body's needs.

How is your mind – is it overactive, always racing around, or is it 'heavy' with negative thoughts? Try to practice being more in the present.

How are you emotionally? Are you in touch with your feelings? Give yourself some time on this.

Have some direction for the year ahead. In terms of your spiritual development, look after your body, give your mind 'a break' by meditating on a regular basis and look at removing blocked energy that no longer serves you due to past wounds.

2nd January

Keep your thoughts positive. Be kind to yourself, as well as to others. Try meditating each day keeping your techniques simple. Start by finding a quiet place to sit, light a candle, burn some incense. Turn off the phone and make sure you will not be disturbed. Focus on your breath, observe the inhale. Observe the exhale. Feel your abdomen rising as you inhale, feel it falling as you exhale. Just simply be with this for several minutes. Be in the present. Try to not let your mind wander. If everyday thoughts come into your mind, try not to engage with these thoughts, let them pass. Focus back on the rising and falling and even saying 'rising' and 'falling' over and over in your mind.

Have a quiet mind, feel any stress or blocked energy leaving your body.

3rd January

Know your body's needs. Eat well – not too much, not too little. If you feel sluggish, then change your diet to lighter foods. Experiment to see what suits you.

A lighter diet would not include alcohol, sugar, red meat, dairy or caffeine. If you do not find this lighter diet easy then perhaps follow this plan for a few weeks and then occasionally have something from the 'heavier' food groups. You may be the type that can have a little of something that you fancy every now and then or you may be the type that is all or nothing.

How is your lifestyle generally? Do you nurture yourself and care about your body? It is not a 'body-beautiful' state to aim for but an inner beauty.

To nurture the Self would be to have treatments such as massage, or to do things that you love and enjoy. Do ensure that some form of body movement is part of your lifestyle to keep your energy clear - some stretching, movement such as walking or regular exercise that you enjoy.

Your body *is* your Temple. It should be cherished, nurtured and respected. It is your vehicle that takes you through your life.

4th January

To keep your energy system healthy and flowing, take regular exercise. This does not mean pounding the pavements with joint-impacting jogging or hitting the local Gym. But taking some energy-shifting movement such as Yoga, Tai Chi, Swimming or Walking. Ideally a minimum of 20 minutes every day combining something like a little cardiovascular, some stretching and strength work to keep the joints mobile and strong and the muscles stretched. Yoga is ideal for most as it is powerful in the sense that blocked energy is removed from the body, but is also subtle as you are working mindfully with the breath. You should work entirely at the level that suits you at that moment. Yoga should be learnt with a qualified teacher. It should be enjoyable. You will do postures, breath work and meditation in a good class. Use your discernment when finding a teacher. They should be emanating peace and calm.

5th January

How are you today emotionally? This means how are you feeling?

As adults, it is difficult to express feelings in a way that is considered acceptable. As children, we could express ourselves more freely. If we hurt we cried; we screamed when angry; we laughed. As we go through adolescence, we learn to 'control' our emotions.

Unless you are freely expressive with your feelings which most are not, adults tend to suppress emotions as it is considered unacceptable to express in ways such as anger and fear for instance. Happy and not showing emotion is allowed in public.

If you have built-up anger or blocked emotions take a walk in nature and find a secluded space. Express your feelings – shout and scream into the vast open space of the sky. Note how you feel after. Another way to express is through Art – drawing, painting, writing, music, singing, dance etc.

6th January

There are four elements of nature which are earth, water, air and fire. These elements are energies also within us. Earth is represented as the physical body. Water is represented as the emotions, air as the mental energy, the mind, and fire as the spirit; your life force.

Take a walk in nature. Open your heart and really feel a

connection with nature. Feel the earth beneath you as you walk. Find a body of water: either a lake, a river or the sea and connect with your emotions. Breathe in the fresh air and let your mind settle and focus on where you are right at that moment, not letting it slip into the past or into the future. If it is sunny, feel the beautiful warmth and healing energy of the sun giving you energy, lifting your spirits. At times walk briskly and feel your energy flowing.

Try chanting the following:

Earth my Body
Water my Blood
Air my Breath and
Fire my Spirit

7th January

Do you have any direction for the year ahead?

Set yourself some realistic goals, work towards your aims.

How do you know where you are going if you have no plans or direction?

This will not be written in stone but will be a few goals for you to achieve. This will give you something to aim for.

Dream your year ahead and see it manifest.

8th January

Are you stuck in any old patterns? Patterns that you may have brought forward from last year perhaps, or from earlier – from childhood. Have you inherited patterns and behaviours from your parents? These patterns could be blocking your energy which will stop you walking forward in life.

Do you feel 'stuck' in life – stuck in a rut?

These patterns could be behavioural issues, control, serial relationship issues, addictions, destructive behaviour, being stuck in your ways of thinking with your beliefs.

Recognise any patterns you may be in and work on them. You

may need the help of a Therapist or Healer or perhaps embark on a self-development course.

9th January

How is your mind today?

Today, is your mind your friend, or your enemy? Is your mind being kind to you? Or is your mind being controlling and nasty. Telling you how down and depressed you are?

Your mind is your Servant, not your Master. Through spiritual practice you will learn to know the Self, you will be in control of your mind. You will understand ego and how too much of this energy can lead you, rather than your true Self, your intuition.

10th January

Are you in touch with your inner child?

Can you play, have fun and laugh? Can you experience joy in your life? Can you maintain joy in your life or does it come and then quickly go again.

Have you the gift of innocence? Or are you too grown up, always 'doing what is best' because that is safe.

Sometimes it is appropriate and life-enhancing to take risks, be The Fool, take a leap of faith and trust that is the right thing to do.

11th January

Do you rest when you are tired? Often we ignore the signs that our mind and body need to rest.

For women, our energy levels change quite dramatically as we go through the menstrual cycle of 28 days which is the same length of time as the cycle of the moon.

For men, tiredness is too often ignored and it is only when an illness occurs that they stop to rest.

Be kind to yourself, if you are tired, then take a rest, put your feet up or lie on the bed, close your eyes and ask The Great

Divine for healing as you rest. When your healing rest is complete, give your thanks.

12th January

Mind, Body, Spirit.

The spiritual triad is made up of the Mind, the Body and the Spirit.

The Spirit is 'AGIB' – A Greater Inner Being. This Greater Inner Being is Spirit – Energy – Consciousness – Soul.

You are Spirit – in a physical body.

If you are 'in tune' you will be in balance. You are following your destiny, your life's purpose. Life is good.

If you are not 'in tune' your Soul will be restless, your Spirit becomes disjointed and out of harmony with the Soul.

13th January

How is life?

If you can answer this by saying 'good, or happy, joyful, contented, balanced, perfect, brilliant, fulfilled, enlightening', then you are following your path with integrity.

If you answer 'How is life' by saying you are 'depressed, blocked, stuck in a rut, ill, taking drugs, taking too much alcohol, unstable, violent' etc, then you would find it healing to start walking your spiritual path.

This means – taking some form of body movement to shift blocked energy, meditating to calm the mind, going for healing, maybe visiting a Therapist, self-study, learn to ground your energies and connect your spiritual energies.

Shamanism can bring you to your centre so you are rounded in life which means being grounded and also being connected.

14th January

Do you live with honesty?

Are you honest with yourself, and to others?

Are you true to yourself? Are you following your dreams? Do you speak your truths? To be honest is to be open. It is better to be honest with others and live your truths rather than live a lie.

Speak with honesty, and speak from the heart, saying what you want to say, rather than what you think others want to hear. Do this in a way that will not verbally harm others.

15th January

Do you know yourself well?

Do you like yourself?

Through personal development you will achieve self-knowledge. Self-study is an important part of spiritual development.

To know yourself is to know your mind, understand your emotions and be aware of your physical needs.

16th January

It is vital to spend some time alone, in order to get to know Oneself.

Try to spend a little time alone each day or even take time out – a day, a week, a month, and a year.

When you are alone, do not have constant stimulation and distraction. Turn off the radio, the TV, unplug the phone and turn off the mobile phone.

Be in silence.

See how that feels. See how your mind is.

17th January

Did you know that your thoughts can be heard? Are you aware that your thoughts carry energy?

Your thoughts are heard by the Universe and if carried with the right intent, can manifest.

An example would be for you to ask The Great Divine 'could

you please send protection to my family with healing energy through this difficult time?'

If you think in your mind that your relationship is over, then the relationship will cease to be working. If you keep on wishing that you could lose weight, be careful what you wish for as you may manifest a sickness and diarrhoea bug which will be a most unpleasant, but a quick way of losing weight!

18th January

If you send out loving thoughts to a situation, then the energy will follow.

An example would be if a friend is going into hospital for an operation, you can ask for all to go well, and for healing to be sent to aid recovery. You sit quietly and imagine the operation going smoothly, you see a beautiful healing purple light around your friend and see them absorbing this healing energy. Repeat this daily.

Observe your friend in their healing process. Let go of any ego and always remember it is the Universe doing the healing, not you, you are the Communicator, the Channel.

19th January

This same theory applies if you think something negative about someone.

Your negative thought will carry a vibration out into the universe and to this person. This will not do any good at all. Try and have compassion for all living beings and just know that people have wounds and baggage and most carry this around with them sub-consciously often and consciously sometimes.

If you have a gripe with someone or there is bad energy in your family, send loving thoughts to these people.

Watch how the energy will change. Watch love and compassion coming back to you.

The mind has a power that draws and attracts energy that you put out – negativity will attract more negative thoughts, positivity will attract positive thoughts.

20th January

If a disaster has occurred in the World somewhere, like a tsunami, earthquake or flood, then sit quietly and send out loving healing thoughts to that situation. Then, do not torture yourself with worry for those involved. Just know that energy will follow your intention of peace and healing. This is the practice of healthy detachment.

This can be applied to war-torn countries where innocent civilians are caught up in gunfire, battles and the horrors of war. Send out loving, healing thoughts to those involved, asking The Great Divine for peace to be restored.

21st January

Be a Spiritual Warrior.

Be empowered and walk in your own power.

Take what you need from Teachers, Gurus, Icons and Religions. Decipher what you think is useless, take the good bits that resonate with you.

It is OK to be eclectic – to take what you need from different religions, philosophies and wisdoms. Some books will provide you with great teachings, but always know that they are someone else's words.

22nd January

A good Teacher will make you feel empowered and help you walk your path.

A Teacher who is not so good will tell you how good they are, will claim to be Miracle Healers and will make you feel you need them. You do not need Teachers of this sort who will take your power from you, and who you will give away your power to them.

It is also not wise to idolise your Teacher, they are another human being, just like you.

Walk in your power, do not allow others to disempower you. This applies not only to Teachers and Gurus but your partners, friends or family.

So use your discernment when finding your Teacher. They do have a habit of appearing in your life when needed. Know when to have a Teacher and when to be the Hermit, to spend time alone being your own Teacher.

23rd January

Cellular memory is where vibrations from thoughts and emotions affect the cells throughout the body. That is in tissue and muscles in your body.

If you ever get tension in your neck and shoulders then perhaps your stress levels are high. Perhaps your mind is sending out negative thought-waves which are received throughout the body. Perhaps you are stuck in negative emotions such as grief, fear, anger, dislike, which will send these vibrations into the body and create blocked energy. We do tend to hold on to past emotions which are then created as blocked energy within the body. Worrying causes more stress so if you are every anxious about a person or a situation, simply ask your Guardian Angel for help, protection and to guide you with non-attachment.

24th January

How can you release this blocked energy?

By practicing energy-releasing exercise movements such as the Yoga postures or Tai Chi for instance.

Through the breath by eliminating toxins through specific breathing techniques.

By receiving energy healing such as Reiki.

Meditation to calm the mind and be in the present.

Looking at negative energy blockages at your heart centre by healing your emotions.

Following a spiritual shamanic path by connecting with nature, connecting with Spirit and connecting with the Self through personal-development.

Finding a good Healer and Teacher to help you get back your power.

Understand the concept of non-attachment.

25th January

Become a Spiritual Warrior.

Seek the Mystery - The Great Divine.

What is your name for the Great Divine?

That Energy that is higher than the Self that you sense, commune with, pray to.

Spend some time today thinking what that energy is to you, what are your truths.

Do you believe in Spirit Guides, The Angelic Realm, The Earthlings such as Faeries?

Within you is Spirit - A Greater Inner Being - AGIB.

You, Spirit Guides, Angels are one with The Great Divine – there is no separation.

26th January

It would be a true Spiritual Warrior that seeks liberation. This liberation is another word for freedom.

Freedom from what exactly?

Suffering. Things that weigh you down in life.

Start eliminating things in your life that cause suffering to you.

Assess those things that weigh you down in life.

Being aware is the key.

Then perhaps a glimpse of enlightenment can be attained.

27th January

A good Spiritual Warrior will live authentically. You will be true to yourself, you will know yourself.

Be who you want to be, not what others want you to be. Sometimes others can put pressure on you in life, for instance to succeed. Success is often measured by qualifications gained at school, prospective career, material wealth, but surely a successful person is one who lives their life with balance and happiness?

28th January

A gift that you have been blessed with in life is that of free will. You should use this free will to help you seek your own truths and your authentic Self.

You will not be able to use your free will if you follow doctrines and dogma, or are obsessive with religion. These are Others' words. Speak your own words, not that of Others.

Walk your spiritual path with an open mind, like that of a child, with trust and innocence. Take on board the things that sound true, use your intuition and rational mind to decipher the truths from the untruths.

29th January

You are on a journey of transformation. An energy exchange will be taking place as you take your journey of life and as you walk your spiritual path. Old blocked energy will be released, toxins expelled and new fresh energy will replace it.

Through actively walking your spiritual path, receiving healing, having therapy, self-study, spiritual development, this is personal transformation. Other helpful tools are Yoga, Tai Chi, Meditation, Shamanic Healing with Journeying and Soul Retrieval to bring back lost energy and the self-empowering Medicine Wheel.

30th January

Do not think that spiritual development is opening up your upper spiritual chakras by developing your psychic abilities and mystic powers. This does not make you a Spiritual Warrior, this makes you a Clairvoyant or Medium which still holds a value but does not necessarily make you a spiritual person as such.

It is less painful to connect with Spirit, see pretty colours, be with the Angels or Faeries, to star gaze, to navel gaze etc, than to look inside the Self, to see not only the light within, but also your dark inner Self, that is quite hidden and repressed.

31st January

Dark within - what is this?

Do not panic, you are human and you are here to experience the Sun and the Moon energies – the light and the dark, warmth and cold, male and female, fire and water, ego and intuition – in other words opposite forces.

The dark within is connecting to those energies which are often deeply hidden and repressed such as anger, grief, fear, jealousy etc. These are blockages to your path and should be appropriately released. Once these blockages are removed, the dark within is a beautiful place of peace and bliss.

Chapter Two

1st February

How do you continue to release blocked energy?

With the help of a qualified professional Teacher or Practitioner such as:

~ Yoga Teacher or Tai Chi Master
~ Spiritual Healer using methods such as Reiki, Angelic Healing, Emotional Freedom Technique etc.
~ Shamanic Practitioner – journeying, soul retrieval
~ Psychotherapist
~ Hypnotherapist

Find out which method is most effective for you.

Ask your Healer what personal development work they have done.

3rd February

Sometimes in life, you will experience:

Anger	Grief	Illness
Fear	Depression	Inflated ego
Materialism	Control issues	Low self-esteem
Abuse	Jealousy	Desires and attachments

These are part of the experiences of life but do not get stuck in this negative darkness, use your will, be free, be liberated, move on, don't repeat patterns and mistakes.

Instead, live with:

Joy	Happiness	Love	Freedom
Laughter	Excitement	Compassion	Bliss

4th February

To help with your self-empowerment, healing and moving on, make a list of those things that annoy you in other people, qualities that irritate you and bring out anger. In other words, things that press your buttons.

Some examples are:

- People who do not listen
- People that talk at you, rather than with you
- Bossiness
- Over-opinionated people
- People who are controlling
- People who whinge all the time
- People that rant

5th February

These are often mirrors to you which means that you probably have these characteristics yourself.

These negative qualities and emotions within you, will affect your energy system.

If you are feeling balanced, are content and are in a state of equilibrium in life, then your energy, your fire, your spirit, your life-force will be strong. You will be containing this energy within your body.

If you are worried, are down or depressed, have repressed anger or irritation, or live in fear, your energy will be leaking outside the body and your life-force will be weakened.

6th February

It is said that illnesses and physical ailments, weaknesses in the body such as stiffness, aches and pains, arthritis etc, are very much linked with the state of mind.

If your mind is calm, your body will feel relaxed and centred. If you are a constant worrier, and are stressed, you will often get an upset digestive system, headaches, inability to relax.

If you lose a loved one and do not give yourself an adequate grieving period which means releasing emotions and honouring this rite of passage which is death, this could lead to conditions such as asthma, hay fever, breast cancer. If you have suppressed anger, this could lead to issues with your liver which is also linked to your digestive system. Anger and/or depression can often follow on from deep grief.

7th February

If you have suffered the loss of a loved one and you dread birthday dates and anniversaries, then do not fear these.

Honour these special days. Celebrate the life of your loved one and cherish your special memories.

Give yourself some time and space to allow any grieving and tears to flow. Do not block your emotions. Be free.

Tomorrow will be another day and you will feel different and that is why you should not suppress your emotions.

Light a candle for your lost loved one.

8th February

The requirements of being a Spiritual Warrior are as follows:

Understanding the Self
Carrying out Self study
Clearing your Chakras
Looking in the mirror of the Self and seeing the light and the dark
Going within, taking an inner journey
Physical focus and discipline
Mind control through Meditation

9th February

Now you are on your path you must understand your Self.

Honour your Ancestors and your culture, your indigenous people and be proud of who you are.

Do you know who you are, where you are and where you are going in life?

Do you have a good balance of your material life and your spiritual life?

Do you feel something is missing in life?

Who are You?

10th February

Walk your walk and talk your talk.

Time to invite you to do some self-study.

Start with looking at your archetypal energies – who you are, your energies. Perhaps start with looking at your horoscope – your birth chart, find out more about your Sun Sign, Moon Sign, Ascendant, which energies you are working with.

Look also at your numerology number to find your birth number – see what energies and vibrations you are working with, what your challenges are. Find out more about your family, who you draw to you, your place of wounding and what lessons you can learn from this (see my book – 'Your Quest for Spiritual Knowledge').

Read sacred texts such as the Yoga Sutras (see my book – 'Your Quest for a Spiritual Life').

Learn about the mind, body and spirit.

11th February

A powerful day for meditation. Find a quiet place to sit, light some incense, burn a candle, turn off the phone.

Take a few deep breaths, letting go of any stress or tension on the exhale.

Focus at your heart and see a beautiful pink lotus flower.

Breathe in a beautiful gold healing energy, and take this energy to your heart.

Exhale rubbish, old blocked energy, stress or any negativity. Continue for a minimum of 10 minutes.

12th February

To be a Spiritual Warrior you should do continuous healing and clearing of your chakras – your main energy centres. Often a colour is related to the chakras. These centres are located up the spine in your body as follows:

Base chakra - red
Sacral chakra - orange
Solar Plexus chakra - yellow
Heart chakra - pink or green
Throat chakra - blue
Brow chakra - purple
Crown chakra - white

By taking the following visualizations you will be helping the energy to clear from each chakra, which allows your inner winds to flow freely. This means you are in a good place of health, physically, mentally and emotionally.

13th February

Base Chakra.

Focus your mind around the area at the base of your body. Visualize the colour red. See a red flower, open up the petals of this flower. The age that affects the energy of this centre is from your birth to around 3-4 years of age.

What do you feel about this time of your life? What energies do you sense? Did you come into this world with loving parents, loving energy?

Take your time and spend several minutes focusing.

When you are complete, visualize the red flower and close down the petals.

Ground yourself by visualizing a big old Oak Tree. See roots going into the ground and see roots coming out of your feet.

14th February

Start your day by sending out love to your family and friends, or anyone that comes to mind.

Sacral Chakra.

Focus your mind around the area below your navel. Visualize the colour orange. See an orange flower, open up the petals of this flower. The age that affects the energy of this centre is from around 4 years of age to around the age of 8.

What do you feel about this time of your life? What energies do you sense or see? These are crucial childhood years and form your earliest memories of life.

Take your time and spend several minutes focusing.

When you are complete, visualize the orange flower and close down the petals.

Ground yourself by visualizing a big old Oak Tree. See roots going into the ground and see roots coming out of your feet.

15th February

Solar Plexus Chakra.

Focus your mind around the area of your stomach. Visualize the colour yellow. See a yellow flower, open up the petals of this flower. The age that affects the energy of this centre is from around 9 years of age to around the age of 15.

What do you feel about this time of your life? What energies do you sense or see? These are adolescent years, the early teenage years.

Take your time and spend several minutes focusing.

When you are complete, visualize the yellow flower and close down the petals.

Ground yourself by visualizing a big old Oak Tree. See roots going into the ground and see roots coming out of your feet.

16th February

Heart Chakra

Focus your mind around the area of your heart. Visualize the colour pink or spring green. See a pink or green flower, open up the petals of this flower. The age that affects the energy of this centre is from around 16 years of age to around the age of 21.

What do you feel about this time of your life? What energies do you sense or see? These are later teenage years, when you fall in love and fall out of love.

Take your time and spend several minutes focusing.

When you are complete, visualize the pink or green flower and close down the petals.

Ground yourself by visualizing a big old Oak Tree. See roots going into the ground and see roots coming out of your feet.

17th February

Throat Chakra

Focus your mind around the area of your heart. Visualize the colour blue. See a blue flower, open up the petals of this flower. The age that affects the energy of this centre is early adulthood when communication skills are being used.

What do you feel about this time of your life? What energies do you sense or see?

Take your time and spend several minutes focusing.

When you are complete, visualize the blue flower and close down the petals.

Ground yourself by visualizing a big old Oak Tree. See roots going into the ground and see roots coming out of your feet.

18th February

Brow Chakra

Focus your mind around the area of your brow. Visualize the colour purple. See a purple flower, open up the petals of this flower. All ages affect this centre.

Tune in to the energies of your mind. What energies do you sense or see? Is your mind your friend, or your enemy.

Take your time and spend several minutes focusing.

When you are complete, visualize the purple flower and close down the petals.

Ground yourself by visualizing a big old Oak Tree. See roots going into the ground and see roots coming out of your feet.

19h February

Crown Chakra

Focus your mind around the area of your Crown, the top of your head. Visualize white, the colour of purity. See a white flower, open up the petals of this flower. All ages affect this centre.

This is where you surrender your will to The Great Divine. What energies do you sense or see?

Take your time and spend several minutes focusing.

When you are complete, visualize the white flower and close down the petals.

Ground yourself by visualizing a big old Oak Tree. See roots going into the ground and see roots coming out of your feet.

20th February

There are energy centres in your feet. Focus on your feet, how do you feel in connection with the earth? Do you feel grounded? Visualize an Oak Tree with roots going deep, deep into Mother Earth.

21st February

There are also chakras above the crown. Focus above your crown, feel the connection to Spirit energies. How does that feel?

When you are complete, visualize the white flower and close down the petals.

Ground yourself by visualizing a big old Oak Tree. See roots going into the ground and see roots coming out of your feet. Chakra clearing is cleansing for your inner winds, your energy.

22nd February

To calm the mind, it is advisable to meditate for around 20 minutes every day.

Meditation will calm not only your mind, but the body also. The benefits are:

- You will sleep better – deeper
- Relieves insomnia – you can use techniques to help you go off to sleep and if you wake in the middle of the night.
- Relieves stress
- Relaxes the nervous system
- Your focus will be improved
- Your mind becomes clearer, clarity replaces confusion
- Opens up your spiritual channels, feel more balanced

Group meditation is very powerful and healing energies can be sent out to the Universe. This will increase the Universal Light and will help to reduce the dark.

Meditation can be started at an early age and is beneficial to all, but possibly not those prone to mental illness and depression.

23rd February

How do you meditate?

Firstly, create a sacred space. Find a space in your home that you could use regularly which is quiet. It doesn't have to be a big space, just big enough for you to sit. Make sure you cannot be disturbed by anyone or by a telephone ringing. Light a candle, burn some incense. Maybe play some meditation music.

Find a comfortable place, preferably sitting. Make sure your spine is straight, without being too rigid. Close your eyes. Allow a few minutes for the body to relax. Ensure your shoulders are relaxed and there is no tension in the neck.

Be warm and comfortable.

24th February

To keep things simple, there are basically three different techniques of meditation. In other words, three different things to focus on:

1) Breath
2) Visualization
3) Sound

These are known as 'objects'.

Use one of these three methods as your point of concentration. When starting meditation, it will help enormously for you to focus on an object and this object can be as stated above – your breath, an image – visualization, or sound – bells, singing bowl, drum or specific relaxation music.

25th February

Today practice meditation by focusing on the breath.

Create your sacred space - see 23rd February.

Close your eyes and concentrate on your breath. Feel what is happening in the body. As you inhale, feel the ribcage moving out to the side, feel your diaphragm lowering, feel your chest rising and your belly expanding.

As you exhale, feel the ribcage coming back in, feel your diaphragm rising, feel your chest falling and your belly coming back in.

Note there are four parts to the breath – the inhale, then a natural pause, the exhale, then a natural pause.

Listen to your breath.

Observe your breath getting lighter and lighter.

26th February

Today focus on a visualization.

Firstly keep this technique simple by focusing on an image such as a flower, a lit candle, a picture with a relaxing landscape, a picture of an Icon such as Buddha, Jesus Christ, an Angel etc. Simple stare at the picture or image and let your breath settle. After a few minutes close your eyes and still try to see the image with your eyes closed, in your 'third eye', your psychic centre.

27th February

Secondly try visualizing yourself in a sacred landscape such as on top of a mountain, on a beach, out in the countryside, walking through the woods or in a garden surrounded by beautiful flowers. Let your imagination run free and if you are on top of a mountain, feel a cool breeze on your face, see the blue sky and feel the vast open space. Feel free.

28th February

Take the visualization technique a step further and use your energy centres, your Chakras as your focus.

Take your focus to the base of your body, visualize a bright red.

Take your focus to the sacral area of your body, below the navel, visualize orange.

Take your focus to the solar plexus, around your stomach area, visualize yellow.

Take your focus to the heart, visualize pink.

Take your focus to the throat, visualize blue.

Take your focus to the brow, visualize purple.

Take your focus to the crown, visualize white.

29th February (leap year)

If this year is leap year, then today use this to reflect over the past four years of your life. What has your journey in that time brought to you in terms of gifts, lessons, challenges?

Chapter Three

1st March

Today is a sound day. Play some relaxation music. See and feel how the energy of this music affects you. See how if effects your mind - what messages your mind sends out to your body. How does this resonate with you. On the internet or even better, find a shop that sells bowls, bells, drums, didgeridoo etc., and spend some time being still, listening to these incredible sounds and how they affect you.

2nd March

Today is a day for Mantra – sacred sound. Create a sacred space and repeat the following Mantras out loud. Do not shout. Just speak the words in a soft and natural way.

Om - repeat 7 times

Repeat saying the mantra 'Om' and this time also focus on each chakra starting with the base. This means take a deep breath in and take your focus to your base chakra. On the exhale say the Mantra Om. Then take your focus to your sacral chakra and inhale. On the exhale say the Mantra Om. Then take your focus to your solar plexus and inhale. Say the Mantra Om on the exhale. Repeat for the heart, throat, brow and crown.

Then repeat the Mantra Om Mani Padme Hum – repeat over and over (pronounced Om manee padmay hum). This is a Buddhist Mantra of Love and Compassion. Firstly direct this Mantra to yourself, then others, then the Universe.

3rd March

Today is a day to focus on being mindful. Sit quietly and set up your sacred space.

Take time to relax the body and then focus on your breath. If any thoughts come into your mind, then do not engage in conversation with these thoughts, just let them pass and they will go. Imagine your mind being still like a pond, crystal clear and perfectly calm.

Spend the rest of the day being present, rather than in the future or in the past. Focus on every task you do.

4th March

Go back to these techniques at any time. Practice techniques that suit you best, there is no right or wrong. Try to make this a part of your daily routine and practice. Eventually meditation will come naturally to you and you will not need a technique as such, you will just 'be' in your meditation.

You will enter 'spiritual time' where there is no time, only timelessness.

5th March

Notice what is happening in nature. As the season changes, observe the new growth in the plant world. Watch the spring bulbs emerging from the earth. The spring flowers depict new growth and the beauty of nature. The depths of the dark winter are now in the past and new life is beginning. Notice the days drawing out - more light hours, more power from the sun. Watch the tree world coming back to life. See the animal world with a spring in their step.

6th March

Take a walk in nature. Observe and reconnect with the plant world. Feel the energy. Stand or sit near a tree, place your hands on the trunk, feel the energy through your hands. Now there is hope – as the end of Winter is drawing to an end, the long, cold dark nights. Spring is near, nature is changing, be in tune with this change. Open your heart – your centre, feel nature.

7th March

Check whether you have correct proportions in your life. Examples are as follows:

Work and creativity
Rest
Play
Family
Relationships

In other words, do not give too much of your energy to one of these. A relationship should be a part of your life, but not rule your life. Work should be a part of your life, but you should give yourself time to relax and have fun away from this energy.

8th March

Do you *let* work rule your life? Does work constantly dominate your thoughts? Can you switch off from work when your working day has finished, or do you allow work to creep into your free time?

Does this affect your sleep patterns? Learn to 'stop' working when you get home. Meditate to help you switch off.

Also earn your living honestly. Then you will sleep well at night. Work because you enjoy what you are doing rather than just for money. When you are out socializing, talk about other things other than work so you can switch off.

9th March

With regard to rest, do you give yourself time to switch off from work? Do you know how to relax? Relaxing is being calm and still and allowing the body to be free of tension. The mind should be also having 'quiet time' and this is why meditation is so useful.

Reading is relaxing, as is watching movies or TV, anything

that allows the body to be still and the mind switched off.

Nurture yourself with relaxing treatments such as body massage.

10th March

With regards to play - are you in touch with your inner child? Do you know how to play and have fun? Who makes you laugh?

Have some 'play-time' – this could mean hobbies and sport so long as you are having fun, and not having any other agenda, not putting pressure on yourself.

11th March

With regards to family, your family should be a part of your life, but not every part. You should give your family your time and energy but at the same time have this in balance with giving your Self time and energy. Family bring you love but can also be demanding and tiring. Get things into perspective.

Assess how you are with your family, do you give them enough of your time, or too much of your time?

12th March

Are you putting too much time and energy into your relation-ships, and neglecting other aspects of your life? Look at specific relationships in your life, such as the relationship with your parents, your partner, your children, friends etc.

Or, on the other hand, are you selfish and not give your relationships enough of your time and energy?

Relationships should be an equal exchange of energy. Give and take will be required, to make them work.

13th March

Putting these parts of your life into perspective will provide a healthy balance. Not giving too much of your energy to one area, or too little of your energy to one area. Look again at the following aspects of your life:

Social – meeting people, laughing and chatting with friends
Family
Rest and relaxation
Work
Relationships
Personal and Spiritual Development
Play, laughter joy and fun

14th March

Today ask your Partner or closest friend how they are feeling. Listen to their answer.

We are often asked 'how are you?' – we answer 'fine thank you'. Of course we are not always fine.

When someone asks 'how are you feeling?' they can really get in touch with their own feelings and emotions. That is how they truly are today.

15th March

Holding Space is a precious gift that you can offer. There are times when your Family, Friend or Client may need to have a rant, to express their true feelings and emotions.

Look at this person, do not speak and listen to what they have to say. It will be very tempting to give your opinion back, to agree or disagree with them.

Holding the space for someone is really listening and giving them that rare opportunity to say what they need to say without being interrupted. This allows them to go deep into themselves, without the energy being dispersed through interruptions.

It is so warming to hear someone actually say 'I hear you'.

16th March

If everyone practiced moral principles, the world would be

kinder and at peace.

Let's look at your attitude to others and the simple vows of life.

Firstly we will study non-violence.

When you speak, are you kind with your words? Do you let anger and violence come into your words?

Are you violent to others? Do you physically hit or enforce pain onto others or an animal? If so, seriously look at that.

Are you violent to the Self? This could be with self-sabotaging thoughts or physically. Be aware of never harming others or our animal friends, or the Self of course.

If you eat meat, be mindful about where the meat has been sourced. Free-range animals will be better energy than factory-farmed animals. The effected energy is in the meat you are eating.

17th March

You should speak your Truth in life. It will take you years to discover what your own truths are. When speaking, talk from the heart and notice the difference to talking from your head.

What you read in books are someone else's words. Resonate with these words that ring true to you.

To discover the ageless wisdom that is within the Self, is like discovering the Holy Grail. Seek, and you will find.

By walking your spiritual path, you will collect bits and pieces in an eclectic style – a bit from religion perhaps, a bit from Buddhism, a bit from Hinduism maybe. When you speak your truths, you will channel the Higher Truth but with your own learnings and teachings.

18th March

Another Vow of Life is not to steal. The Karmic Police will catch up with you, if you intentionally take what is not yours and deceive another.

In your work place, be mindful of ethics. If you rip folk off as you carry out your daily work practices, expect the same back. Earn your living honestly.

It is shameful to steal other people's possessions. It will not make you feel good in the long run.

Are you a taker in life? Do you take all the time – money, energy? Try giving for a change.

Some folk can drain you as if they are taking your own energy so be aware of this.

19th March

Practice the rule of moderation. This can be applied to say intake of food – not too much, not too little. Also to alcohol – one or two drinks is fine a couple of times a week, any more than four times a week is rather excessive.

A little chocolate or sweet treat every now and then will not harm you at all.

Do you over-exercise – are you hooked on adrenaline or do you have a good balance?

Are you over-sexed? Do you have to have sex every day? If yes, then the balance is not right.

20th March

Do you have greed under control? This would be having the willpower and knowledge to know when you have enough of something.

This can be applied to food – knowing your own body's needs and realizing when to understand correct portion size.

With money, greed can often get out of control. Know when to stop, sit back and enjoy what you have in terms of materialism, rather than continuously chasing more and more, bringing excessive tiredness and misery.

21st March

In the Northern Hemisphere today is the Spring Equinox.

Welcome this beautiful time of year into your life. Celebrate by going out into nature observing the changes taking place. Watch the plant world sprouting back to life.

Close the door on Winter and be mindful of any projects you would like to develop. Now is a good time to put your energy into something creative and 'give birth' to new ideas.

Everything will look green so connect with your heart energy centre. When you breathe, breathe in the beauty of nature.

22nd March

Now look at your attitude towards the Self, your self-discipline.

With regard firstly to cleanliness – how clean is your body – and your mind? Outer cleanliness means keeping the physical body clean by your daily washing routine.

Internal cleanliness means trying to keep the body free of toxins by exercising and eating a healthy, balanced diet.

Also by meditating regularly, you will have a healthy mind. If you have a healthy mind, your emotions will be more balanced, resulting in a healthy body.

23rd March

How content are you in life? Are you happy with your lot or do you yearn for better possessions, to be in a better relationship, to desire a move to a bigger house, drive a nicer, flashy car?

Whilst some ambition and fire energy is healthy, be aware that constantly desiring these things leads to discontentment.

Look around you and count your blessings, be aware of the gifts you have in life, appreciate what you have.

It is possible to be content with very little. The more material possessions you have the harder you have to strive in life. Having enough, will be harmonious.

Happiness comes from within.

24th March

How are you with discipline? This can be applied to many areas of your life. For example discipline with your exercise routine, discipline with your diet, discipline to study and take your spiritual practices such as regular meditation.

Too much discipline can lead to control and missing out on enjoyment in life. Too little and you will not move forward in life – you will take one step forward and two steps back.

Discipline should be in balance, as should lots of areas in life.

Beware of 'Belief Systems' that are dictating to you, with so much discipline and rules, you may forget to be happy.

25th March

Have you ever spent any time studying your Self? It is interesting and useful to study your archetypal energies which are your astrological signs and your numerology number (my book Your Quest for Spiritual Knowledge will guide you).

To know yourself truly you should also study sacred texts such as Patanjali's Yoga sutras (see my book Your Quest for a Spiritual Life).

Self-study also involves freeing the past wounds that restrict you now through self-development. The Shamanic way will empower you and find your true Self. Shamanism is being in balance with the Spiritual World energies and Mother Earth energies which meet at your heart centre. Unblocking the energy that holds past wounds through Shamanic healing will bring you to your centre, will bring back your power and help you live your life in harmony and balance.

26th March

Has it every occurred to you that there is an energy out there that is greater than yourself? Find your own name for this energy. Some suggestions are – The Great Spirit, the Creator, The Great Divine, The One, The Great White Spirit, God. This energy is not particularly Male or Female but is a Great Consciousness.

As for your earth life, there is no one who is more powerful than you. You must walk in your own power, find your own truths, understand the Higher Truth – Wisdom within you.

Following doctrines and dogma means you are giving your power away.

27th March

Spiritual ignorance means you are walking your earth path asleep.

At some point in your life, you may think there is more to life, you feel empty, unfulfilled. You look around you and see your family who you love, your work that you should enjoy, a roof over your head and sufficient food on your table.

But you have a pang inside you that says there is more – you are right, there is more.

If you are in spiritual ignorance you will not find your authentic Self, your life will pass not knowing the truths, bliss and enlightenment.

Incorrect comprehension clouds your perception, leaving a feeling of dissatisfaction.

28th March

Your ego is the Male energy within you. It is the part of you that forms your personality, the part of you when you state 'I am'.

If your self-esteem is high, then your ego will be strong. If your ego is overly inflated, then your opinion of your Self will be rather overly high. Also you think you will be right all the time, you try to be better than anyone else and compete with other people.

It is important to have high self-esteem but not an inflated ego.

Ego is your fire energy – too much and you will get burnt, too little and not enough energy – weak life force.

29th March

If you have too little ego, your self-esteem along with your confidence will be low. Your fire energy will be lacking.

You will have no ambition as you will lack the fire to drive yourself and fuel your self-confidence. Your opinion of your Self will be rather unkind, your saboteur within will rule your thoughts.

Spiritual evolution from self-development, attending courses, healing etc. will result in the authentic you. Your ego will be in its proper place of renunciation with the Self.

Your Male and Female energies will then be in balance and your inner winds will flow freely.

30th March

Do you desire things that you know deep down you either cannot have or should not have?

An example of something you cannot have is to desire a new car or new television because your existing one has been upgraded with a new model but there is absolutely nothing wrong with what you have. Purchasing this new model would put you in debt so the constant desire should be curtailed as in the long run it will only bring misery.

An example of something you should not have would be desiring a piece of chocolate cake which you give in to and then suffering indigestion from the overload of sugar in your system.

Learn to detach yourself from these desires.

31st March

Do you carry with you hatred and anger? It is very unhealthy to contain these energies within.

You must learn to let go of hatred towards someone in particular. These energies can manifest in the physical body in the form of illnesses such as arthritis so do not internalize these energies. Let go in appropriate surroundings and circumstances.

A good way to release anger is to take yourself in the middle of a field or place where there is no one to be seen. Just let go of anger by shouting and screaming or making primal noises to release this negative energy.

If your anger is deep-seated due to years of suppression, you may need to see a professional therapist to release it.

You will feel so much lighter and more powerful for it.

Chapter Four

1st April

Fear is another block to your spiritual path.

At one time or another in life, you will experience fear. For example as a child, fear will stop you doing dangerous activities such as jumping off a wall that is too high which may cause you injury.

Other fears such as fear of death, fear of the Spirit World, fear of getting old etc. will not serve you in any positive way. It is not healthy for the mind or body to attach yourself to such fears.

Fears in the form of phobias such as fear of the dark, fear of spiders, snakes etc. can be overcome with the help of professionals.

2nd April

How is your connection to nature today?

Find some time to take a walk either in the park, or out in the countryside.

Note the further changes to nature – the beautiful spring flowers. Take some time to smell their scent. Stop and be still. Take in everything around you.

3rd April

An egg is a symbol of New Life! As a chick hatches out from an egg, new life emerges.

Spring is a time of rebirth. Connect with this energy, this fresh energy. Welcome Spring, welcome rebirth. This is a time to close the door on old energy and bring in new energy.

Look around you and see the earth re-birthing as Spring flowers emerge, nature is active and fresh. Underneath the Earth, there is much activity waiting to emerge.

4th April

Find a quiet spot to sit out in nature or create a sacred place in your own garden. This can be a place for you to visit often and can be now known as your 'sit-spot'.

When you sit in this sacred place, give yourself time to settle and relax. Feel the cool breeze on your face. See the beautiful spring flowers. Watch nature coming alive again. Notice any wildlife.

Close your eyes and just feel. Imagine an egg being hatched and connect with this symbol of new life. Feel fresh energy. Feel alive.

5th April

If possible go back out into nature where you will be alone and chant the following:

Mother I feel you under my feet
Mother I hear your heart beat
Mother I feel you under my feet
Mother I hear your heart beat
Hey a Hey a Hey a Hey a Hey a Hey Oh
Hey a Hey a Hey a Hey a Hey a Hey Oh
Hey a Hey a Hey a Hey a Hey a Hey Oh
Hey a Hey a Hey a Hey a Hey a Hey Oh
Repeat several times and connect to Mother Earth.

6th April

Think of the word 'Honesty' and how it sits with you. Meditate on this word.

You should always be honest in your speech so that you can state your truths and others will know where they stand. Be clear in what you are saying.

Also, you should always be honest with your Self. In order to be happy and fulfilled in life you should walk your path being true to yourself.

Then you are living authentically.

7th April

Today try a form of Meditation using visualizations so get yourself warm and comfortable in a quiet space.

Visualizations are a technique that help to focus the mind.

Try various techniques of visualizations. Let your imagination go wild and creative.

For example, visualize yourself out in what would be a sacred place to you – like a beautiful landscape in nature for instance, on top of a mountain, in a forest, lying on a beach, swimming with Dolphins etc.

Play music if it helps and be free. Let yourself go on a Journey in your sacred place of visualization. If your mind flickers back to everyday thoughts, then bring it back to your visualization.

8th April

Be in touch with the Spirit of the four directions - North, South, East and West, and also the Centre, Above and Below.

If you connect these directions together with the intercardinal points, a circle will be formed. This circle becomes a representative of a map of life – and is known as 'The Medicine Wheel'.

'Medicine' means healing, energy, life force. It helps you to see life more clearly. The Medicine Wheel is an empowering method of healing.

9th April

To start your Medicine Wheel, find eight stones. These could be stones that are pebble-size that you can find on the beach. They could be crystals or simply stones that you come across whilst out walking that catch your eye.

Contemplate on where you will find these stones and make it

your mission to seek these eight stones – one for each main direction of North, South, East and West and one for each of the inter-cardinal directions of South East, South West, North West and North East.

These stones are now part of your own Medicine Wheel and are sacred.

10th April

Find a space in your home where you can lay out the stones in a circle – small or large, it does not matter.

Try and get hold of a compass or get an idea of the directions of North, South, East and West. Place each of your stones on a cardinal direction and form a circle. This is now the stone allocated for that direction and represents the aspect which means for instance South stone represents your emotions and inner child.

11th April

Sit and contemplate this Medicine Wheel.

Ask yourself if you feel ready to receive this medicine. If 'yes' then sit and visualize this circle of healing.

See if you feel drawn to a particular element i.e. air, water, earth or fire.

You are made up of these elements and one may be more dominant within you depending on your energies within and this comes from your date of birth. For instance if you are an Aries, you are a Fire Sign, Taurus – Earth, Gemini – Air, Cancer – Water, Leo – Fire, Virgo – Earth, Libra – Air, Scorpio – Water, Sagittarius – Fire, Capricorn – Earth, Aquarius – Air, Pisces –Water.

12th April

Today find out a little more about yourself and your archetypal energies with particular reference to the elements. This is part of your make up that forms you, your energy. Your energies are also made up of the following:

Genetic inheritance from Ancestors.

Conditioning from parents and Elders.

Environment you were brought up in.

Your horoscope sign and your numerology number for your date of birth.

This is a way of discovering the Self and what your challenges in life are.

The internet will give you more details of Astrology and Numerology.

13th April

The South on the Medicine Wheel.

Contemplate the South first as this is the place of the child within you. This is the place of trust and innocence and your childhood years.

There would have been playful and happy times but also times of sadness, incidents and where any wounds whether physical, mental or emotional, would have affected your energy – your life-force.

Spend some time today contemplating your childhood times and see what comes up and how that makes you feel. We often 'bury' childhood emotions and the energy sits in our sub-conscious and unless dealt with, will follow you round the wheel.

14th April

With your focus still in the place of South on the Medicine Wheel, connect to the element of Water which represents your emotions.

Try and be by water today maybe the ocean, a river, canal, lake, or if that is not practical, then bathe in water or visit the local swimming baths and immerse yourself in water.

Get in touch with your emotions, how you are feeling. Observe how your feelings are ever-changing.

15th April

The North on the Medicine Wheel.

This is the place of the adult, the element of air which is linked to your mind – your mental energy.

Take some time to sit and contemplate how your mind is today.

We are too often thinking about the past or the future and not enough time is spent just 'being'. This means being and living with awareness. Being in the present moment.

Meditation practice will calm your mind. When your mind is still, you are open to the truths of the Universe.

Try not to overload your mind with beliefs, lists, chores, stress, full diary etc.

16th April

Today, connect to the element of Air.

Take yourself outside and feel the air on your face. Breathe in and out deeply a few times. Fill your lungs with air.

Make a mental note of how often you say 'I think' rather than 'I feel'.

Observe the birds and see the effects of wind as they fly.

Sit and contemplate yourself as an adult, your relationship with your adult Self.

Then sit and meditate on your breath. Just focus purely on your inhale and your exhale. Notice how your breathing changes the more you relax. Hear your breath. Feel your breath in your body. Notice how the chest rises and falls with the inhale and the exhale.

17th April

The West on the Medicine Wheel

The West is the place of Earth and is represented by our physical body.

This is the place we visit when we do deep inner work – self-development and soul searching. It is the place of dark and is where we touch when we go into 'cave mode'. Just like a bear that goes into a cave to hibernate.

Deep emotional work can be done here and issues and wounds such as death will be dealt with here. This relates to our feminine energy which is our female, dark, intuition, cool energy.

18th April

Connect to the element of Earth. Take an 'earth-walk' – go out into nature. Try and escape buildings, people, noise.

Feel the Earth beneath you as you walk and take in the beauty of nature.

Find a place to sit, and contemplate your physical body and how your relationship is with your physical Self. Do you respect and nurture your body, providing correct nutrition and nourishment?

Reflect upon your relationship to the feminine within you, your relationship to your deep energy within, the dark, and how in touch you may be with your intuition.

19th April

The East on the Medicine Wheel

The East is the place of Fire which relates to your Spirit, your life force, your creative energy, your passions, light, ego, male energy. The East is the opposite polarity to the West.

This is the place of transformation whereas the West is gestation. This is where you will find the energy for you to transform ideas into action.

The Sun rises in the East and sets in the West.

Are you creating what you want from life?

20th April

Connect to the element of Fire. Light a candle or have a fire and sit round it and contemplate the flames, feel the energy, the heat, see the energy around the flame.

If the sun is shining, feel the healing energy, absorb the warmth into your body, how good does that feel?

Practice a candle meditation:

Prepare yourself and the space around you as before. Light a candle and place just in front of you. Just simply watch the candle and fix your gaze. Notice the energy around the flame and how the flame dances around. Close your eyes but still see the candle in your third eye. Imagine within you a light the size of the flame of the candle. Now see this flame gradually growing within you. Keep with this until the whole of your body is filled with this flame. Stay with this for a while and see how this feels to be connected with your fire within.

As a separate practice, prepare yourself and the space around you for meditation. Visualize yourself outside in nature in a landscape where the sun is shining. This could be sitting on top of a mountain, lying down by a pool or lying on a beach with the sun shining down on you. With each breath you breathe in breathe in the energy of the sun. Notice the natural pause after your in-breath. Visualize a healing and energizing yellow energy with each inhale. Breathe this energy into your body. Practice this for several minutes still picturing yourself in your chosen landscape, with the sun shining down on you. After a while visualize your whole body filled with this vitalizing energy which makes you feel as if you are full of fresh energy, full of health and vitality.

21st April

This form of healing known as 'The Star Maiden's Circle' unravels life issues, will show us the source of them and guides us to a place of power where we can make changes.

22 April

The South East on the Medicine Wheel

The South East is the place of our Ancestors and our history.

The South East is the place where we come from in the Spirit World through our Ancestors, our bloodline and into our Earth life, born into a physical body and into a family where we can learn, evolve and meet our challenges in order to become whole.

Your Ancestors, your parents, are your bloodline. They will reflect qualities in you. Some will be good and are real gifts, some more challenging.

Parents obviously have a massive impact on us as individuals. Your inner dialogue which is part of your ego Self will be influenced by your upbringing and conditioning by your parents. This inner dialogue will at times be your friend and at other times your enemy, your saboteur.

23rd April

Take a few healing minutes to reflect firstly on your Mother's bloodline and then secondly on your Father's bloodline.

Write down each of their strengths and gifts. Then write down their challenges and burdens. See how this reflects in your Self.

Contemplate your inner dialogue and how you treat yourself. Are you kind and friendly, or are you unkind and quite horrid?

24th April

The North West on the Medicine Wheel

The North West is the place of habits, patterns and routines that have developed from your upbringing. This is called baggage. Some of these habits, patterns and routines will still serve you and some will not but you are perhaps not aware of this on a conscious level but part of you no longer needs these but your ego will be hanging on.

It is believed that we all have Karma which is family Karma and personal Karma. Personal Karma would have come from actions from past lives. Also from actions made in this life. If your intention is genuine and one of kindness and generosity, then you will be rewarded with the same as that is what you will attract. If you harm others with actions or words and your intention is unkind, then you will attract that back.

Family karma comes in the form of patterns of behaviour for instance that can be released, for instance addictions, controlling behavior, being caught up in dogma and beliefs that give you no free will, taking on parents' traits and behaviour that do not serve you spiritually.

25th April

Make a list of your useful patterns such as being prompt, daily routine of cleanliness, eating habits and routines etc.

Then make a list of patterns that are no longer useful to you such as:

Being a people pleaser
Control issues – letting people control you, or you controlling
    other people.
Depression
Addictions
Being judgmental
Obsessive cleanliness
Eating disorder
Too giving to others
Being a Victim
Being a Rescuer

26th April

The South West on the Medicine Wheel

The South West is the place of Dreams and Archetypal energies. This is where you will plant the seeds of your dreams in your mind, your desires, ambitions, your goals in life. Being opposite the North East on the Wheel where you will find the energy within to manifest your dreams.

Archetypal energies are the energies within you and are affected by your date of birth which will provide you with vital information on your horoscope – your Sun sign, Moon sign and Ascendant, and also your numerology number which is again taken from your date of birth. It is really helpful to get your birth chart done by an Astrologist to find out the energies you are working with, your archetypal energies, to see your own strengths and weaknesses.

Are you the type of person that follows your dreams and reaches fulfillment?

Do you feel you lack the fire energy to get you following your dreams?

27th April

Make a list of your fulfilled dreams in life.

Make a list of your unfulfilled dreams in life.

Can you realistically make any changes to turn unfulfilled dreams into fulfilled dreams?

28th April

The North East on the Medicine Wheel

The North East is the place of choices, manifestation of dreams and how you choreograph your life. It is also the place of balance – of male and female energies and how we need both. The choices that you make and have made in the past will design your life. This is where you will or will not as the case may be, have the energy to follow your dreams, desires and goals and manifest them, making your own choices in life.

29th April

Make a few notes on the way you have designed your life and the choices you have made that do not serve you, that do not bring you happiness and joy.

Write down anyone who has influenced you – were you trying to please them?

Make some notes on the way you have designed your life and the choices you have made that *do* serve you and bring you joy and a sense of well-being.

Examples of how you have designed your life are environment – your choice of place to live, your choice of partner in your relationship, your choice of friends, career, money to a certain extent, places you travel to etc.

Now looking at your Male and Female powers, do you feel in touch with your Male side – ego, your outgoing side, the Sun – the light, self-esteem, confidence?

Do you feel in touch with your female powers – the Moon – the dark, the deep feminine within, your intuition?

30th April

How do you feel about your use of power? Do you feel you walk in your own power? Or do you feel you give your power away to others?

Do you feel you take others' power away from them?

Chapter Five

1st May

Tune in to the wonderful and natural energy of nature. This time of year is traditionally known as 'Beltane' – the time when the plant world is most active. There is a burst of energy and fertility also in the animal world. Time to dance around a Maypole (or watch others!) – celebrate new life and fertility, appreciate nature. Spend today with friends celebrating, be joyful and share food together.

Light a fire in the evening, and ask Grandfather Fire to transform your energy, to give away your old energy, to let go of old issues and to bring in new energy.

2nd May

This is a really active time for wildlife and some species are feeling the effects of the abuse of Mother Earth. In particular Bees.

If there were not sufficient amounts of bees to pollinate plants, the plant world would suffer.

If there were not a sufficient amount of plants, both the animals and humans would suffer.

There would be insufficient food to go round.

3rd May

Now you have let the energy and teachings of the Medicine Wheel settle a little, place your stones in a large circle preferably with a compass or if one is not available then roughly place each of the eight stones on the cardinal and inter-cardinal points. Make the circle big enough for you to sit in. Either write down a few key points or hold them in your memory such as South – Inner child, wounds, emotions, North – Adult, Air, Mind, West – Earth, physical body, dark, deep within, intuition, East – Fire,

Spirit, life-force, passion, creativity, light, South East – Ancestors, South West – Dreams and Archetypal energies, North West – Karma, patterns, habits, routines, North East – Choices, manifestation of dreams, choreography of life, balance of Male and Female.

Enter your Medicine Wheel at South East, the place of the Ancestors and sit in the middle facing the South Stone. Speak of an issue that you bring to this healing circle and how you feel hurt by it. Either speak out loud or to yourself. Connect deep with your inner Self. This is the neurotic circle. Examples of issues are for instance 'why do I not get on with my Mother/Father?', 'why do I hate responsibility?', 'why do I not deal with death very well?', why do I have trouble with intolerance?', 'why am I so angry?' etc.

Give yourself time.

This is your neurotic Self which means there is a part of you holding on to habits, routines and issues that no longer serve or help you and your true authentic Self wants liberation and freedom and detachment from the issues that hold you back.

Afterwards, write down key points to help you remember. Exit at the place of the South East, the place of Ancestors.

4th May

Go back to the centre of your Medicine Wheel entering in the place of the South East, the Ancestors. Sit down and face the South West.

Ask yourself ' With regards to the issue that I brought into the circle yesterday, how does this issue reflect in everyday life and how has it affected my life?'

Again either speak out loud or to yourself and give yourself several minutes to answer the question. Afterwards write down any key points and leave the circle at the place of the South East, the Ancestors.

5th May

Return to your circle of stones and enter at South East, the place of the Ancestors. Sit down and face the stone that represents West.

With regards to the issue, speak of any 'if onlys' you may have.

Connect with your Inner Child and ask yourself 'who does this part of me blame, other than myself?'

6th May

Return to your circle of stones and enter at South East, the place of the Ancestors. Sit down and face the stone that represents the North West.

Regarding your issue that you brought to the circle, speak of familiar recurring patterns in your life. Speak of the habits and routines relating to the issue.

Speak of any 'shoulds' and 'oughts' from this issue that you feel limit you.

7th May

Return to your circle of stones and enter at South East, the place of the Ancestors. Sit down and face your stone that represents the North.

Ask yourself ' what are my beliefs that keep this issue alive?'

'What are my beliefs about Myself and life?'

8th May

Return to your circle of stones and enter at South East, the place of the Ancestors. Sit down and face your stone that represents the North East.

Ask yourself 'what choices have I made that keep this issue alive in me?'

'How do I design and choreograph my life to be the way it is?'

9th May

Return to your circle of stones and enter at South East, the place of the Ancestors. Sit down and face your stone that represents the East.

Ask yourself 'how does having my life this way keep me safe/stuck?'

'With regards to my passion and spirit, what does not get expressed in the way I live with regards to the issue?' Return to the circle of stones and enter at South East, the place of the Ancestors. Sit down and face your stone that represents the North East.

10th May

Return to your circle of stones and enter at South East, the place of the Ancestors. Sit down and face the stone that represents the South East.

Ask yourself 'how do I feel about myself? How is my relationship with myself?'

11th May

Now time to go around the Star Maiden's Circle again but this time as your authentic Self rather than your Neurotic Self.

Return to your circle of stones and enter at South East, the place of the Ancestors. Sit down and face your stone that represents the South East once more.

Ask yourself 'what does your wounded Self need from you?'

State what you need from Yourself out loud, examples are – courage, love, compassion, power, confidence etc.

Now close your eyes and focus on your breath. Take a few deep breaths. Receive from yourself those things that your wounded Self needs from you. Breathe these things into yourself and empower yourself.

Take your time and then move to the South when you feel ready.

12th May

Sit facing your South stone and ask yourself 'how does it feel now to receive these things in my life?'

13th May

Sit facing your South West stone and ask yourself 'how does my life feel now? What are the new possibilities I now open my life to? What dreams am I manifesting and wish to manifest?'

14th May

Sit facing your West stone in your Medicine Wheel and ask yourself 'how does this affect me in my everyday life? How does it feel to live this new dream and way of life?'

15th May

Sit facing the North West stone and ask yourself 'what are my new positive practices and habits?'

16th May

Sit facing the North stone and ask yourself 'what are my new life-affirming attitudes towards myself and life?'

17th May

Sit facing the North East stone and ask yourself 'what new choices do I now make to manifest my dreams and new possibilities?'

18th May

Sit facing your East stone and ask yourself 'how does this new way of being affect my life force and presence in life?'

19th May

Sit facing your South East stone and ask yourself 'how does this leave me feeling about Myself now? How is my relationship with myself now?'

20th May

See how you feel today.

Do not try to over-analyze your experience of The Star Maiden's Circle.

You can repeat this exercise with another issue at any time. You can either do it in stages or do the whole exercise in one go which usually takes between one and two hours.

21st May

If you feel tired during the day, then when practical, take a rest. Close your eyes for at least ten minutes. Try to not let your mind chitter-chatter. Focus on a calm visualization such as a perfectly still lake.

Take several deep breaths and let go of tension as you breathe out.

22nd May

Once you start healing the Self, you start healing your bloodline, your Ancestors.

Patterns will be released and therefore Karma will be released.

So you are not only working on the Self, you are healing your bloodline.

23rd May

If you feel you have been through a particularly intense period of healing and self-development, then let your energy settle before you do any more work.

24th May

Take the opportunity today to rise early. At first light, listen to the birdsong, let it speak through you.

This is a special time of day. Your mind has been still during your sleep time. Now is a good time for Meditation.

Meditate on this beautiful time of year, the beauty of nature with the colours and scents of blossom. Give your thanks for the beauty of life itself and being here to experience another day.

25th May

Through the practice of Meditation your mind becomes still. You can detach yourself from your thoughts and memory.

When your mind is still, your body is still. This state of relaxation is very healing to your body – your nervous system is calm, your heart rate slows down, you are at peace and experiencing harmony.

26th May

There are times in your life when you will feel like you are in a state of confusion. Around you erratic situations will occur and people will irritate you. Life can then feel upside down.

Just know that this will not last.

You will find your truths, find peace again and get back to your centre.

Clarity will replace confusion.

27th May

From day to day your mind will fluctuate from negative – painful thoughts, dark, self-sabotaging ideas and thoughts to positive – light thoughts, happy ideas, kindness, love and compassion to the Self bringing brightness and light.

Your thoughts are effected by your lifestyle, environment, people in your life, career, food, alcohol and drugs.

28th May

To take drugs before the brain has properly formed which is around the age of 21, is the road to self-destruction.

Any recreational drugs are toxic to the mind, body and spirit.

Drugs affect your outlook on life, take away your direction and drive and are used to escape from the inner Self.

Alcohol and nicotine are drugs and are highly addictive. Taking drugs is not a fast-track to spiritual experiences.

29th May

There are five classes of movement of the mind which are as follows:

Right knowledge – a proven theory which has been reliably sourced.

Wrong knowledge – assumptions and presumptions.

Imagination – fanciful or imaginary knowledge which could include delusion.

Sleep – knowledge based on sleep and dreams.

Memory – recollection of thoughts from the past.

30th May

Right knowledge is gained from words and actions of Spiritual Teachers - by joining a Yoga Class, going to Meditation Groups, finding a suitable person who you believe is coming from the right place (is this knowledge their own interpretation, or is it true?). Your teacher should be someone who you feel comfortable with, they should be approachable and when they teach they should be sharing their knowledge with you and not preaching. You should feel warmth in their presence. Use discernment when choosing your spiritual teacher and follow your intuition.

After being with your Teacher, you should feel empowered.

Right knowledge is based on spiritual intelligence, intuition, actual testimony from sacred texts and scriptures or direct from The Masters in Spirit through channeling. Channeling philosophy can be done by those who have mastered the gift in linking to The Great Masters in Spirit.

31st May

Wrong knowledge is caused by error, misconception, or by mistaking one thing for another i.e. you see a bird out the corner of your eye and believe it to be an eagle. You look closer and find that in fact it is a pheasant. From a glimpse you made an assumption rather than being patient and sure and seeing it for what it is. Wrong understanding and wrong knowledge will generate blocks on your spiritual path. Your perception will be clouded and your feelings will be unsettled.

Chapter Six

1st June

When words are spoken, we can often jump to conclusions. Our imagination takes over, leading us to conclusions which may have no substance and this is a sign of weakness of the mind.

When in the presence of your Teacher, allow words of wisdom to sink in. Try and digest wise words and allow them to be, without analyzing everything and making your own assumptions. Let the true depth of these words come through and then, the truth can become clear rather than truths without substance. When a Master speaks, listen, do not try and think about a reply or analyze the words, or judge, just listen and absorb.

2nd June

Lucid Dreaming is a state of consciousness where there is an absence of thought-waves, but there is still a trace of consciousness. When meditating, you should not fall asleep, 'sleep is sleep' and 'meditation is meditation'. (Saying by Theravada Buddhist Monk in Thailand).

Sleep is where the state of consciousness is in a place where everyday thoughts do not clutter the mind but where dreams take place. Not all dreams are prophetic but some are and carry powerful messages.

3rd June

Memory is a recollection of past experiences and words.

These experiences continue to live within you and these can be both positive and negative. Our conditioning from the past is imprinted in our memory and that is why we find it difficult to break old habits. Past experiences may not be forgotten in the mind but they can be healed from the soul. Cellular memory is where emotions are stored in the cells of the body, for instance in the muscles and it is believed that by stretching the muscles through Yoga postures, that releases take place.

4th June

Renunciation is the practice of letting go of your desires and passions. Letting go of your attachments is liberation of desires. This will result in yourself being in a more peaceful space, the mind not hankering after desires but being content. These desires could be in the form of material possessions, foods that you crave but do not really need such as another piece of chocolate, wanting to move house if there is nothing wrong with where you are, buying a new television just because a new model has come in when there is nothing wrong with the one you have. The desires could be coming from the ego and another example is wanting to possess the psychic powers without the right intention. These desires will distract you from your true spiritual path as they are not the goal and these powers alone will not give you liberation.

Let your deep inner knowing lead you and not your ego.

5th June

Non-attachment is being free, being your true self with no distractions. According to Yoga philosophy, the whole of nature consists of three qualities known as The Gunas – Tamas – heavy, inertia, Rajas – energetic, lively, vibrancy and Sattvic – light, luminosity, serenity. We can apply these three qualities to our mind (heavy, lively, calm), to our physical body (inertia, energetic, balanced), and this applies to the animal kingdom, to the plant kingdom, food etc.

Letting go comes with self-development by understanding these qualities of nature within the Self.

An example would be, what makes your body and mind feel heavy. Let's take a certain food that you know makes you feel heavy, this would usually be too much red meat, dairy, alcohol, caffeine or sugar? When you consume this heavy-type food, then the body will be in a heavy state – lethargic. When you eat high energy food such as convenience foods, quick fix sugary foods, then the body will be all over the place – fidgety. So when you eat light food such as vegetables and fruit, the body and mind will feel lighter. When you are in tune with the Self, then the soul can be seen and you will then be working at a deeper level, free from attachments. Then you will be in a more balanced space.

6th June

The more time and energy you put into walking your spiritual path, the more you will get out of it.

If at any time you reach a state of harmony and balance and you feel blissful, then keep going with your self-study, reading the sacred texts and meditation.

7th June

Reflect on the idea that today is the last day on this planet and tonight you will die.

How does this feel, how does this affect you?

Is there anything you wish you could have done in life?

Why put off things you would like to do, why not make plans to do something, such as a trip to India, climb a mountain, sky-diving, bungee jumping etc. It doesn't have to be crazy, it could be something simple such as visit an elderly relative, ride a horse on the beach, make up with someone you have fallen out with, stay up all night and watch the stars.

8th June

If your mind is particularly muddled, you can't think straight, you can't focus on any one thing as there is too much buzzing in your head, then try the following:

Make sure your home is uncluttered.

Go for a walk out in nature.

Spend time alone – a few hours, days, weeks.

Each morning, start the day with a meditation focusing on your breath. Concentrate on your nostrils and focus on your inhale first and secondly focus on your exhale. When you breathe in count your breath and when you breathe out also count your length of breath. Make sure you are using full length of breath available to you. Now try and make your exhale longer than your inhale. For example inhale for count of five and exhale for count of nine. Practice this for several minutes.

9th June

If you ever feel that stress has spiralled out of control then try one of the following:

Take some time away from work and your normal environment.

Take some regular exercise – it really does work!

Try a gentle Yoga class.

Make sure you have time for your creative energy to be used.

Meditate using simple techniques

10th June

Today and everyday tune into your body. Spend time 'scanning' your body. Be still and silent and prepare yourself and your space for Meditation. Lie down and take time to make sure your whole body is relaxed.

Take your focus to your head area and reflect on how your mind is today.

Bring the focus to your neck and shoulders and see if you feel tense. If so, roll your shoulders back and down and relax.

Bring your focus to your chest area and feel how the energy is around your lungs and heart. Feel the chest opening as you inhale.

Bring the focus to your stomach and feel how your digestion is.

Bring the focus to your lower abdomen, the reproductive area. Scan further down the body to your hips, upper legs, knees, lower legs, ankles and feet.

Really take your time.

Then do not particularly focus on any part of your body, but still have the awareness within. Just see where your mind is drawn to in your body and when it settles at a place take a deep breath in, and when your breathe out imagine you are letting go of any blocked energy, stress or pain. When you breathe in you are breathing in a healing energy and when you breathe out you are breathing out blocked energy, toxins, waste product, pain – really let it go.

11th June

Repeat the above and then take it a step further.

Now take your focus deeper than your physical body and to your energy body which is also known as your spiritual body. This energy runs through channels in your body and is your life force. Visualize the seven Chakras up you spine.

Other words for this energy are:

Prana - (Hindu, Yoga)
Chi - (Chinese, Tai Chi)
Ki - (Japanese, Reiki)

12th June

When you are meditating it is quite an interesting exercise to practice different hand gestures or positions. Examples are as follows:

Place your hands on your lap with your palms facing down.

Place your hands on your lap with your palms facing upwards.

With the back of your hands resting on your lap, bring together your thumb and index finger.

With the back of your hands resting on your lap, bring together your thumb and middle finger.

Bring together your thumb and ring finger.

Bring together your thumb and little finger.

Rest one hand on your lap in front of your body, palms facing up, place one hand on top of the other.

This will connect you to your energy system – Prana, Chi or Ki. Each of these different hand gestures will affect your energy system in different ways as follows:

Palms facing up – receiving energy.

Palms facing down – going inwards.

Bringing thumb to index finger – calms your mind as it links to mental energy.

Thumb to middle finger – releases blocked energy around your heart.

Thumb to ring finger – calms liver energy and digestion.

Thumb to little finger – Calms energy in small intestine in the lower abdomen.

13th June

Your breath is linked to your energy, which is linked to your mind, which is also linked to your body.

This means that when you have kind loving and peaceful thoughts, then your breathing also becomes calm and regular.

When you are anxious or stressed your breathing is irregular and shallow.

14th June

When you came into this world you came in with an in-breath.

When your time has come to leave your body and leave this

world, you will go out with an exhale – a last breath out.

As living beings we can go for a while without a drink, days without food but we cannot go without air – breath.

15th June

Notice that there are four parts to the breath:

Inhale
Natural pause
Exhale
Natural pause

Focus on your breathing and observe these natural pauses in the breath.

When the breath is still, everything in your body is still.

Listen to yourself breathe – hear the breath and feel the breath – it is very relaxing and meditative.

16th June

Instead of always focusing on the inhale first then the exhale second, try it the other way round and this is how it is practiced in Tibetan Heart Yoga.

Concentrate on your nostrils and focus on your exhale first and secondly focus on your inhale. When you breathe out say 'one' and when you breathe in say 'two' as follows:

- Exhale 'one'
- Inhale 'two'
- Exhale 'one'
- Inhale 'two'
- Repeat this over and over for several minutes as it helps to calm the mind, bringing you back to your centre.

17th June

Take some time today to observe what is going on with nature. Summer Solstice is approaching – the longest day and shortest night. Nature is in full bloom and at its most active. The days are long and the evenings are light.

This is a beautiful time of year.

Relate this to your Fire energy and see how your energy is today – is it high, low or in the middle in a balanced place. In other words, how is your life-force? Lack of healthy life force will leave you feeling tired and at this time of year in theory your life force should be strong.

18th June

When you are taking your meditation practice, always prepare your space around you – switch off the phone, light a candle, 'light some incense, making sure those you live with know not to disturb you. Then prepare yourself by sitting in a comfortable position, making sure you are warm, take a hand gesture and give yourself several minutes to relax by focusing on your breath to help you focus your mind.

Make sure you use full capacity of your lungs when you breathe, the full length of breath available to you, being very relaxed, not forcing the breath. In today's world where folk are so stressed and busy, they even rush their breathing!

19th June

Why not take today to clear out clutter.

Start with your home environment and have a tidy up first. If your home feels cluttered, have a sort out. Put old ornaments and books that you haven't read for over six months into boxes and take them to a charity shop.

Sort out your clothes and again give those clothes to charity that you no longer wear. See how good that makes you feel.

Notice your mind and how de-cluttered that has become

already.

20th June

Tomorrow is Summer Solstice and traditionally folk would have stayed up all night tonight.

Try doing this, taking provisions and a blanket with you and visit a sacred site such as Stonehenge or Avebury or a stone circle near you.

See the next morning in and watch the sun rise.

This is a beautiful special experience that you will never forget.

21st June

Today is the longest day of the year which means the most amount of daylight hours where the sun is at its most powerful.

This is exactly the middle of the year, six months previous was the Winter Solstice as will be six months ahead from now.

Take some time today to celebrate perhaps with friends, share food, fun and laughter.

22nd June

Take some time today to reflect on the last six months. Think of challenges that have come your way, lessons that have been presented to you. Write them down in a journal.

Have you learnt from these challenges and lessons? Acknowledge and put these behind you.

See today as a threshold for moving forward and on to the second part of the year.

23rd June

Take a nature walk – out in the countryside, by a river or canal, along a coastal path or in the park.

Connect with Mother Earth, with nature. See and feel this beauty. See how alive nature is at this time of year.

Feel that aliveness within you.

24th June

Even on sunny days, we can sometimes feel low or depressed.
Do not despair, there is help out there for you!
Seek a professional as follows:

Aromatherapist – will use bespoke oils that are mentally and
emotionally uplifting.

Counsellor or Psychotherapist – will listen to you.

Shamanic Practitioner – will work with mind, body and spirit
to shift blocked energy with treatments such as Journeying
with the drum, Soul Retrieval, healing with the Medicine
Wheel.

Spiritual Healer – will use energies such as Reiki, Angel
Healing, Crystal Healing and is very relaxing and calming.

25th June

Shamanism is Yourself walking in your own Power, being
connected to Mother Earth, nature and also being connected with
your Higher Self – Spirit. Shamanism is being in balance and
walking with your energies in harmony spiritually and earthly in
other words in both worlds.

There is no Guru to give your Power to, for you are the Guru.

26th June

There will be times in your life when you will learn from a
Master or Teacher. This is how we learn and progress. Do be
aware that every Teacher is simply teaching their truths and ask
yourself if what they are saying resonates with you. Listen to
their words. Are they words of wisdom or is this wrong
knowledge?

Is this Teacher preaching to you or sharing knowledge? Is
their knowledge from a belief system or is this true?

Do you feel empowered after being in the presence of your Teacher?

This is where it is so important to use your discernment.

27th June

There will also be times in your life when it is appropriate to be the Hermit. Have no Teacher for the time being. This is especially true if you have spent much time reading spiritual books, seeking knowledge, attended courses, have had healing etc.

You should give yourself time to let all this energy settle. This is when you will have Self-Realizations.

If it is possible, spend time alone. Other people can often be a distraction. It is very healing to have periods of solitude and silence.

28th June

Try and make today a theme and focus on 'Water'. Today drink lots of water to cleanse your body.

Take a walk by water such as the ocean, a pond, a lake, river, canal. Then take several minutes to stand or sit by the water. Feel this energy of water within you and connect to your emotions. How are you on an emotional level today?

As you carry on drinking water, let your emotions run through you.

Go for a swim or if that is not possible, take a long relaxing bath or a refreshing shower.

Feel cleansed.

29th June

If you do not let your emotions flow through you, then this energy becomes stuck. This results in unhealthy blocked energy. It can then build up to making you feel as if you could explode with rage or anger which could erupt at inappropriate times.

Then your emotions are internalized which is very damaging

to the mind and body. Your mind will become clouded and confused and you may become irritable.

Let your emotions be in motion, flowing like a river.

30th June

Today go out in nature and seek an Oak Tree and take with you an offering such as tobacco, nuts, seeds etc.

An Oak Tree symbolizes wisdom and spiritual growth. It is the Tree of Courage and the doorway to inner strength. They are extremely slow-growing which shows us patience. From little acorns, grow huge Oak Trees and two most important qualities to enable you to walk your spiritual path are discipline and patience.

Sit at the foot of your Oak Tree with your back leaning on the trunk. Visualize the huge roots going deep into Mother Earth. Feel this grounding energy. Let go or ground any issues you may have on your mind and ask Mother Earth to expel your negative energy.

Give your thanks and offerings.

Chapter Seven

1st July

Be in the Present.

This is practiced by Buddhists worldwide.

Keep checking your mind. It will want to wander back to the past or it will try and skip to future thoughts and events.

Very rarely will it be in the present moment. Make today particularly a day of bringing your thoughts to the Now. To live with awareness is very centering. To curb the multitudinous straying thoughts that constantly cloud our mind will take discipline and energy.

2nd July

Occasionally in life, circumstances such as an illness or injury forces us to be still. Instead of seeing this as a time of frustration, getting pointlessly angry, see this as a time that you have been called by The Divine to rest. Make yourself as comfortable as possible and take the time to read, to be creative and try writing. Express yourself with words, maybe poetry.

Know that your recovery time will come and you will resume your busy life.

3rd July

All the different religions and philosophies of many cultures all point to the same little gem.

This applies whether they be Christian, Islam, Kabbalah, Buddhism, Hindu etc. In reality there should be no conflict with each other, they are merely different paths to take which are influenced by culture and upbringing.

They all describe the same inner realities.

4th July

Energy follows thought.

When there is a disaster such as 9/11, the Tsunami or the Haiti earthquake, the collective consciousness is one of grief and sadness as people around the world hear of the news.

Once the initial shock has taken place, if people could send out their love and healing on a worldly scale, then this energy is powerful as the mind consciously sends this positive energy out. Suffering can be relieved.

Spend today sending love from your heart centre to a person or a situation. Without getting emotionally attached.

5th July

The mind is so powerful.

There are parts of the mind that if accessed, can awaken magic powers. These powers can be used for dark, as well as light, it is your choice.

If collectively these powers are used in love and light, then the planet would be a harmonious and beautiful place to be.

If these powers are used in a dark manner – for increasing personal ego, power and wealth, then the planet will be destroyed, the human race will end and life on Earth cannot be experienced.

Live in love and light.

6th July

Today is the birthday of who is considered to be, the only living Avatar, The Dalai Lama.

His Holiness the Dalai Lama works in service to Buddha, in love and light. He spreads the message of peace. To live with inner peace and to live with peace around us.

He is a true example of living by spiritual laws. He speaks the Higher Truths and emanates Divine Love.

7th July

These Spiritual Laws are:

- Non-violence in speech and actions.
- Speaking the right truths.
- Do not steal.
- Live simply and with moderation.
- Non-greed – do not keep desiring.
- Keep the body cleansed daily and also the mind cleansed by meditation.
- Live with contentment, if you keep having desires, it will bring you restlessness and misery.
- Read sacred texts and discover inner wisdom. Practice self-study by exploring your archetypal energies, astrological energies, numerology, look at your inner male which is your Light and your inner Female which is your dark.
- Find your devotion, faith, trust to The Great Divine – The Great Spirit – or an energy greater than yourself.

8th July

Sometimes you will meet someone who has an impact on you in a positive spiritual way. In their presence you will feel Divine Love, you will see beauty, an inner beauty.

They will move with their feet touching the Earth for they feel Mother Earth energies.

Their eyes will see. They speak their own truths.

This beauty is a reflection of You.

9th July

When you see a quality in someone that irritates the hell out of you, maybe this quality is a reflection of something within you.

When you see a positive quality in someone, something you admire, this is also a reflection of you.

10th July

Some days you will feel like you are chasing your tail.

You will be surrounded by chaos, your mind is spinning out of control, your blood pressure is pulsating, your head feels like it might explode.

This is when you will least have the desire to meditate but this is when you will most need it. So you will have to give yourself a nudge as you will benefit hugely from meditating.

11th July

Good intentions alone, are not enough and will not do. They must be backed up by good actions.

You should take your spiritual path and journey with the right intention and be vigilant and diligent.

If not, your practices will slip, you will find excuses for not taking your practice and before you know it, life gets in the way.

12th July

Regular effort and practice will result in a more balanced mind. Peace will be in the mind, will be felt in the heart, the body will be more in harmony.

The Soul will be obtainable.

This means that you will get to know the Self, the authentic You.

13th July

To know Thyself is to know God.

Your God can be perceived by whatever you are comfortable with – The Great Divine, The Great White Spirit, The Greater Energy etc.

This God energy is within you. When you partake in spiritual practices, you will get in touch with the God within you.

14th July

It is one thing to keep saying 'I must take time to meditate' or 'I must start a Yoga or Tai Chi class' or 'I must go for a walk in nature'.

It is another thing, to then follow this up with good action. Then discipline will come into play even more, to sustain these practices and make them a part of your daily life and routine.

15th July

Like The Devil card in the Tarot depicts, within us all are animal instincts.

Self-discipline is not suppressing these energies of lust, greed, sexual desire, delusion, jealousy, anger, but taming the brute within. This means humanization of the animal and spiritualization of the human.

Your brutal nature should be worked with and destroyed so you can work in the Light with your divine nature.

16th July

Work to be free from:

Passion, anger, selfishness, abhorrence, egoism, materialism, greed, jealousy, prejudice, behaviour patterns, mental patterns, criticalness.

You may need help from Therapists, Shamanic Practitioners, attend workshops, courses.

It will be like peeling layers of blocked energy away – to discover the centre of bliss and balance. Buddhists liken this to an onion – peeling off layer by layer to reveal the core – the centre, without all the baggage.

17th July

Ways to find liberation:

Self-development

Self-study

Seeking help from a Therapist or Healer – Shamanism is very
    powerful and effective

Yoga

Meditation

18th July

Self-development – a good start is to read spiritual books such as
'*Your Quest for a Spiritual Life*' and '*Your Quest for Spiritual
Knowledge*' by the Author.

Attend workshops and courses. Use your discernment and
find what energies you are drawn to.

Self-study – find out who you really are.

Seek counsel from someone who has had similar experiences,
preferably a qualified Practitioner.

Join a development group – often a Teacher comes along at
the right time.

19th July

Self-study – discover who you really are – your gifts and
burdens.

If you have a birth chart done, you will have more knowledge
of your archetypal energies. Find out your numerology number
from your date of birth (see my book 'Your Quest for Spiritual
Knowledge'). The more you look into this the more you will find
out about yourself which can only help you through life if you
understand your reason and purpose, and how you have used
your free will in life.

20th July

Seeking help from a Therapist – there are many therapists out
there, some better than others. There are also plenty of therapies
out there and some suit some folk but not others.

Some people take to talking therapies such as counseling and psychotherapy. Others want harder hitting powerful therapies such as shamanic healing where you will take a journey of visiting your inner world, your wounds and remove the energy that has been blocking you and retrieving the energy that you have lost making your life force stronger and helping you to be in your own power.

Some people believe that you can reach enlightenment through regular meditation practices.

Different courses for different horses. You will be drawn to the therapy that your soul is seeking. Visiting your past and looking at your wounds takes time and is not something to be cleared in one session, it can take a few, several or many depending on the therapy, the therapist and you but there are no rights or wrongs or rules, you go with how you are feeling.

21st July

Spiritual Healers do not actually heal you. They are channels that pass energy through.

If they make such claims and revelations then stay clear. For they are in ego and not working in pure intent.

This Divine Energy that is channelled through, will go to where it is needed and your higher self will know what to do. The more work you do on the Self to clear blocked energy, the clearer you will be as a Healer. Regular clearing of own chakras is essential as a Healer.

22nd July

Divine Energy is called many different things such as:

Energy
Chi
Ki
Prana

It is all the same thing – energy. This energy is within you and every living thing. It travels through channels in your body known as meridians or nadis. This is your life-force, your Spirit Body.

Energy travels through your chakras and is also outside your body known as the aura.

This energy is part of our breath, when you breathe in you are inhaling fresh energy. When you are breathing out you are exhaling toxins and waste products in the breath which are expelled from the body.

23rd July

This aura consists of energy of different forms, different layers.

There is your physical body, your mental body and your emotional body.

The physical body is affected by the food and nutrition you put into it, exercise and rest and relaxation.

You mental body benefits from meditation to calm this energy down.

Your emotional body is affected by your feelings of present and past.

Past lives are imprinted in this energy field.

24th July

The Soul is eternal and comes into a physical body for an incarnation on Earth. You could be a young Soul, or an old Soul which means you would have had many lives.

You may have had lives spanning over centuries. That is why it is wise to take spiritual development – so you can evolve at a Soul level.

Past life regression is a therapy to take you back over previous lives to help with an issue or challenge with your present life. It is one thing to be told of a past life and another to be actually regressed.

25th July

When you follow a spiritual path in life, your internal light will shine bright – your Soul.

Being in touch with your Soul will bring you:

Truth
True happiness
Balance
Bliss
Sometimes known as:
Enlightenment.

26th July

Within you is this Consciousness – Soul. Outside the Self is the Great Consciousness – The Great Divine, The Great White Spirit, God, Buddha, Allah.

But there is no separation.
All is One.

27th July

Today, go out to your regular 'sit-spot' in nature or find a space where you are alone. Sit or lie on the ground. Close your eyes.

Imagine roots going in to the Earth. Breathe in this energy. See rocks, crystals. Repeat many times.

Then on an out breath, take your focus above your Crown, then above your Crown and then up to the Clouds.

Feel the balance of the two energies.

28th July

Try being in tune with your Sun energy - your Divine Male energy that reveals who you are outwardly, your personality.

Find your Divine Sun energy by playing some loud music that you believe would help you tune in to your Male and outgoing side. This side of you being heat, outwardly appearance, fire, spirit, life force.

29th July

Try being in tune with the cycle of the Moon. Note how your emotions change as the Moon cycle changes.

You are the Deep Feminine – you are the Goddess, the nurturer, the carer, the intuitive, the Dark and the cool energy.

Find your feminine energy within.

Play some music that you feel will help you – maybe soft feminine music or drumming if you finds that takes you into a relaxed and deep place. Take an intention of finding your deep feminine energy, relax and see what visions and feelings come to you.

30th July

It is important to keep a journal whilst you travel on your spiritual path. It is very healing and therapeutic to write down your feelings and changes of mood, record dreams, write down or draw your visions. You will come back to this journal time and time again.

31st July

Today go out in to nature and find two small tree branches or sticks. One will represent your male and one female. Whilst you are out in nature, also pick up anything that you come across such as feathers, leaves, cones etc.

Take your female branch and decorate it with your findings from nature. Also write on strips of paper anything negative to do with your deep feminine that you would like to release. Attach these strips of paper to your branch and repeat several times. Decorate the branch with ribbons, colourful wool etc.

Repeat for your Male side and tomorrow you will go out and burn your craft.

Chapter Eight

1st August

Find a place where there is a fire going or light a fire yourself. It doesn't have to be a huge roaring fire, small is fine.

With the intention of 'giving away' your blocked female energy within and getting back your lost energy, place your Female 'Give Away' on to the fire. Be expressive – if you need to shout or cry or really release, then do so.

Then take a few minutes to compose and let the energy settle. Repeat the same exercise for Male by placing your Male 'Give Away' on to the fire and release any blocked Male energy, again being expressive by releasing emotions.

Let the energy settle and then give thanks to Grandfather Fire.

2nd August

Take today as a day to rest as much as you can. Reflect on your ceremony of yesterday and write down your feelings and experiences in your journal.

Then just try to 'Be' today.

3rd August

This is a time of year known as 'Lammas'. It is time to reflect back to assess your year to-date. Reflect on challenges and lessons and what you can learn. A time to meet with friends, share food and laughter.

Lammas is a time of year to celebrate the beginning of the harvest season. It is the middle of Summer. The Sun's strength will gradually start to wane and the plants are starting to wither and drop their fruits. It is time to experience a sense of abundance but at the same time start planning ahead for Winter to come to make sure there are enough fruits and grains stored.

4th August

Also see this concept of storing and planning for ahead in terms of your energy. Do not expel all your energy, store some for up to Christmas and the really dark and sometimes harsh months of January and February.

This time of year also sees continued growth of crops and fruit and accept that this is part of the cycle of death and rebirth.

5th August

The Moon has three phases:

The Waxing Moon – the phase from New Moon to Full Moon – the illuminated area increases every day.

The Waning Moon – the phase during Full Moon and the next New Moon. The illuminated area becomes smaller. This is the Crone aspect of the Goddess, the energy is waning.

The Full Moon – is shaped like a complete disc. The Moon's illuminated side is facing the Earth. This is the Mother form of the Goddess – full power.

The New Moon occurs when the Sun and Moon are in conjunction, occupying the same part of the sky from the viewpoint of the Earth. This is the Maiden form of the Goddess and is also known as the Crescent Moon where the energy is growing.

The Moon rises 50 minutes later each night so it sometimes rises during the day and can be therefore seen during daylight hours.

6th August

The Sun is the Star at the centre of the Solar System.

The Sun orbits the Earth hence our different seasons.

At this time of year the energy is still powerful but is starting to wane each day.

By being in touch with the Sun cycle and points of the year such as the equinoxes, you will be in tune as your Ancestors were.

7th August

Leo is the Sun sign at the moment. In nature the fruit is now sweet and juicy and delicious to eat.

From within, express your Self – your inner child, be spontaneous, be creative, feel and alive and love yourself and love life.

Let others feel the energy of your sweetness within.

8th August

Abundance – look around you – see the abundance – it is there. In nature there is abundance of fruit for harvesting, there is water for cleansing, the Sun for warmth and light, the Moon for dark and coolness. There is beauty everywhere.

Spend today being positive, with positive people who share your love of nature and life.

Share some food with someone whose company you feel an abundance of love and uplifting energy.

9th August

Today is a day of self-nourishment. Nourish yourself with only loving and positive thoughts.

Practice some nourishing meditation bringing in love to your heart chakra and sending out love.

Practice some nourishing breathing techniques. Try the humming breath by taking a deep breath in and as you exhale hum like a bee gently and softly using each energy centre up the spine as a focus point starting from the base, sacral, solar plexus, heart, throat, brow and crown.

10th August

Take the next few days to remind yourself of the Eight Limbs of Life:

Code of conduct - non-violence, right speech, not stealing, moderation and non-greed.

Vows of life - cleanliness of body and mind, contentment, self-discipline, self-study, devotion to a Higher Energy.

Movement of the body in the form of stretching and exercise.

Correct breathing.

Connecting to your Inner World.

Concentration techniques.

Meditation.

Living in balance and harmony.

These limbs of life are reminiscence of the Buddhist eight fold path.

11th August

If you live in accordance with these eight limbs you will radiate inner beauty. This will show to the outside world – they will see and feel the beauty of clear fresh eyes, beautiful skin, and healthy body. From the inside they will feel your beautiful energy radiating from you for your light, your Soul will shine bright.

'Then the Soul is a lamp whose light is steady, for it burns in a shelter where no winds come' – The Upanishads – a sacred text.

12th August

By continuing your practice of meditation, you will attain a healthy mind.

By continuing self-study, healing your wounds, clearing blocked energy, your emotions will flow freely and in a healthy way.

By continuing to eat well – not too much, not too little and know your own body's needs in terms of nutrition, your body will be healthy and free from disease and illness.

Healthy mind

Balanced emotions
Healthy body
Healthy spirit

13th August

By continuing these practices your Soul becomes obtainable. You will have a sense of connection, knowing. Life starts to have a new meaning, death is not feared. You will be free from desires. You know who you are, where you are going in life. You understand your challenges and will have Self-realizations which you take note of. You can detach from your neurotic Self and live with authenticity.

'To know Thyself,
Is to Know God'.

14th August

It is good to know what this Greater Power means to you and for you to use your own terminology. Youngsters today shy away from the word 'God' as they associate this word with the Church, boring sermons, preaching, Sunday school, and the Bible.

Other words to consider are:

The Divine
The Great White Spirit
The One
The Higher Power
The Great Energy

15th August

It is always interesting to check what is happening on an Astrological level – with the planets, The Solar System.

Everything is affected by the movement of these planets and the changes that take place. Since time began, humans have looked to the heavens for guidance.

The Zodiac is a band of stars that encircle the Earth. This band is divided up into the 12 signs of the Zodiac. This circle of stars rotate every day. With the movement of the Sun, Moon and Planets this creates a different sky pattern for each moment in time.

16th August

It is very interesting to get your birth chart done by an Astrologist. The three most important astrological indicators of character are:

Sun sign
Moon sign
Ascending sign

Sun signs show what we want in life, what we are trying to become.

Moon signs show what we need in life and how we interact emotionally.

Ascendant points the way or shows the path we need to follow to balance the qualities or potential of the Sun and Moon signs. How we see the World. As the Sun and Moon signs indicate parental influence – the Male and Female energies that have effected and influenced us.

17th August

Astrology will help you to understand the Self, the character from your natal chart. It can also help with relationships and health. It is a practical tool to enhance your well-being.

It can help with business decisions and career guidance. It helps you understand your personality, your emotional needs and help you to recognize your strengths and weaknesses.

Synastry is relationship analysis and Astrology can point out those who are compatible to yourself and those who will present more challenges.

18th August

Try to make today a cleansing day. For every cup of tea or coffee you have, drink a glass of water. This will help guard against dehydration and will flush out the toxins from your system.

Try to limit your caffeine drinks to no more than 3-4 per day. Do not take a caffeine drink after 6.00pm. Increase your intake of water during the day. Filtered water is good and better for the environment than water in plastic bottles.

Perhaps try a new fruit or herb tea and find one that you like.

19th August

It is imperative to get a good night's sleep. The following will help:

Do not eat or drink late.

Practice meditation daily to calm the mind.

Take some form of stretching or body exercise daily.

Do not go to bed stimulated.

Take a few minutes to read before sleeping to help switch off.

Make your sleeping environment comfortable, be warm and relaxed, tidy etc.

Have some rose quartz and/or amethyst by the side of your bed as it is calming energy and you will absorb this into your body.

Sprinkle a couple drops of Lavender onto your pillow.

Play relaxation music.

20th August

If you wake up in the night and cannot get back off to sleep then try not to engage with thoughts and chitter-chatter of the mind as this is obviously stimulating. As you lie in bed, in your mind repeat a Mantra which is one of the fastest ways to stop everyday thoughts coming into your head when your mind wants to be active. A Mantra is a sacred sound.

Inhale deeply and on the exhale, chant 'OM' in your mind. Repeat this over and over many times.

Then chant the Mantra 'OM MANI PADME HUM' pronounced 'OM MANEE PADMAY HUM' on the exhale, in your mind. When you breathe in focus around your heart area and when you breathe out focus on the Mantra. Repeat this over and over many times. This is the Buddhist Mantra of love and compassion.

If Mantras fail to get you in a sleepy state then I suggest getting out of bed and sit on a cushion on the floor beside the bed making sure you are keeping yourself warm. Focus on your breath and let your mind settle. Be patient, this will take many minutes. When you feel yourself getting sleepy, crawl back into bed and sleep. This works every time!

21st August

Chanting Mantras – sacred sounds take you into silence. By chanting Mantras either out loud or in your head repetitively you will go into silence, into the void. This silence is communion with The Great Divine.

This silence is freedom and liberation.

22 August

How is your inner voice today?

Is it a Saboteur telling you unkind things about yourself, ripping you apart, tearing your self-esteem down? Is it negative and dark?

Or, is your inner voice kind, telling you how great life is, how great you are, recognizing your achievements, boosting your self-esteem?

23rd August

Are you a 'Rescuer?'

Do you take on people in your life and try to 'heal' them, try to run their lives for them, take on their troubles and woes and make them your own troubles and woes? In other words take on their responsibilities.

Or are you coming from the other side – are you a Victim? Do you try and get others to make decisions for you? Do you let others take your responsibilities in life? Are you controlled by anyone? Are you a 'Poor Me'.

Hopefully you are not either. You are someone who takes full responsibility in your life, not a Rescuer and not a Victim.

24th August

Isn't it sad that some folk compromise their own health for the sake of vanity? Why would you do that?

Rather than visit their inner world and confront issues and fears, some hide behind a mask of make-up, fake tan, Botox, plastic surgery.

How can this be justified, even looking at its ridiculous facts in terms of money when there are folk in the world that have not even got enough food each day or a roof over their heads and then there are those who will spend thousands on plastic surgery for pure vanity.

All this does is radiate fakeness and shallowness.

Inner peace and beauty radiates to outer beauty.

25th August

I once asked a very varied group of men what and who their ideal woman would be. They all pretty much came up with the same reply which was 'a woman who loves herself for what she is'.

In other words someone who is comfortable in their own body, who has a peaceful, positive mind and therefore who is in touch with their own feelings.

Not someone who is neurotic about their body has a restless mind with constant desires and who is emotionally unstable.

26th August

When you wake up and rise in the morning, give your thanks to The Great Divine for simply being alive – what a great gift this is.

Welcome the new day in, whatever the weather. Acknowledge that the Sun cannot shine all the time, Mother Earth also needs rain or she becomes dry and parched.

Take a gentle stretch and know that life is precious and give thanks for the joy of living.

27th August

Some of the joys of being alive are:

Rising to challenges
Enjoying the countryside and nature
Food
Sex
Exploring other cultures and countries with travel
Having a career that fulfils you
Seeking the Self
Enjoying and appreciating the wonderful blessing of being alive on this planet
Appreciating life and abundance around you

28th August

There will be signs in nature of Autumn slowly approaching. So today find a place out in nature perhaps your regular 'sit-spot' in the park, garden or out in the countryside.

Take your shoes and socks off and feel the earth beneath your feet, really connect to Mother Earth. Feel how grounding that is. Breathe Earth energies into your feet and into your body.

Be alive, connect to your senses, smell nature, see the beauty around you, hear birds and sounds of nature, feel the fresh air and connect.

29th August

Have a think about what makes you feel good such as:

Being with like-minded people
Going for beautiful walks
Spiritual practices such as Yoga and Meditation.
Reading a good book
Exercise
Eating healthily
Watching a good movie
You don't have to spend much money to feel good.

30th August

Think about those things that weigh you down in life and do what you practically can to eliminate these things, such as:

Stop spending money, especially if in debt
Push yourself to do things such as take a walk, if you are
    depressed, get out and about
Change your diet if you worry about your weight
Don't drink alcohol if it gives you a headache and makes you
    feel lousy
Move on from people that constantly harass you and give you
    aggro

31st August

One of the most addictive things is actually sugar.

Have a day of absolutely no sugar. Check every product you consume including breakfast cereals, sauces and salad dressings. You will be surprised at the amount of products that contain sugar.

Sugary foods are comforting foods but be aware that sugar is highly addictive. Obvious sugary foods are chocolate, candy, jams and puddings. Not so obvious food groups are alcohol, gravies, table sauces, salad dressings, snacks, spreads.

It would be wise to check labels and then try a week without sugar and then longer. See how that makes you feel.

Chapter Nine

1st September

An invitation to spend today looking at your diet. Check for patterns and habits within your diet that are no longer serving you, for example you have to have eight cups of coffee every day, you have to have a chocolate bar after dinner, you have to have two sugars in your hot drinks.

Your taste buds get used to certain foods. Try cereals that are healthier and free from sugar. If dairy upsets your digestion, switch to soya, you will soon adapt to the taste and it is very easy on the digestive tract.

Do you need sugary desserts to follow a meal? Try switching to fresh fruit or yoghurt.

Eliminate sugar from tea and coffee – it is a habit that you can break and will be better for your teeth as well as your general health.

2nd September

Do you have an odd glass of alcohol because you simply enjoy it or do you need it?

Folk drink often to make themselves merry, as they believe they appear more social and funny to be with after a few drinks. Often the reverse is the truth – people who drink can often become loud, raucous and over-social.

People often drink to suppress feelings and emotions – to push these energies deeper into the Self.

Alcohol often brings out the worst in people and the pain of poisoning the body and bad behaviour can mean a downer afterwards.

It is best to leave the alcohol and deal with the blocked energy.

3rd September

Note the changes out in nature. There will be signs of a change of season approaching.

Changes happen all the time in life as the circle of life goes around and around. Do you go with these changes and allow new energy to flow or do you resist changes creating energy blocks?

4th September

How grounded do you feel today?

Take some time to ground your energies. Be still and allow yourself to feel connected to Mother Earth.

Breathe her energies into your body and take your focus deep into Earth. See yourself as an Oak Tree, with roots going deep, deep, down into Earth.

5th September

The Great Mother is Mother Earth.

She will nurture you, feed you, hold you and love you.

She is the positive Dark Energy and will take you to your inner world. Know who you really are, find your truths and wisdom.

She is the keeper of your Soul – your essence, You.

6th September

The Great Father is Father Sky, the Sun, the Light, and the Cosmos.

Whereas The Great Mother is your Deep Feminine, the Great Father is your Divine Masculine – how you present yourself to the outer world, how others see you.

7th September

Problems are often presented to us in life and instead of making a mountain out of a molehill, turn the problem into a challenge.

Try not to let the problem weigh you down, take some time to be logical and positive and how this issue can be overcome.

Overcoming challenges will make you grow as a person and will strengthen your character.

8th September

Do something today that uplifts you. Maybe watch a feel-good movie.

Spend time with a positive uplifting person.

Go for a walk in nature and breathe in fresh air.

If it is practical, visit the seaside or walk by a river.

Do something that makes you feel good.

9th September

What is your relationship with your body like at this moment in time?

How many people do you know that only speak of what they consider to be bad things about their body?

Are you happy and comfortable with your body? What don't you like and what do you like?

Could you make changes such as introducing exercise?

If you are a little overweight, does it matter? It only matters if it bugs you, is a danger to your health or stops you doing things you would normally like to do.

10th September

Yoga is one of the most effective ways of being in touch with your own body. A good Yoga class consists of:

Postures – which should be accessible, comfortable but at the same time provide you with some stretching and strength work. If you feel like you are participating in a gymnastics class a suggestion of finding another class would be a good idea.

Breathing – breathe properly and efficiently, using different
techniques.

Meditation – to calm the mind.

Once you start your Yoga journey it generally invites you to look
at your lifestyle, your diet as you feel you want to nurture
yourself with good food, take some movement to keep your body
healthy and participate in regular practice.

11th September

Today is a day to remind yourself that we should have respect
for other religions and cultures. Terrorism does not solve
anything or help causes. It simply brings pain and havoc in to
innocent people's lives.

12th September

Make today a day of giving of your time and love.

Visit or call someone to cheer them up.

Maybe write a letter or card to someone you have not seen in
a while.

Send some flowers or a nice gesture.

It is beautiful to receive a spontaneous gesture or gift from
someone.

There are plenty of Takers in the world but not so many
Givers.

13th September

Spend a little time today being in the presence of an animal. Be it
a bird, cat, dog, horse or even an insect. Observe this animal and
link in with their energy. Let them speak to you.

Animals are instinctive and intuitive. We can learn so much
from them. They are messengers from the Spirit World and they
can communicate with you if you let them.

14th September

If you feel like starting your spiritual path is like climbing a huge mountain, then do not despair. Set yourself small challenges and lifestyle changes to start with and gradually build it up.

Do not be harsh on yourself, treat yourself with love and kindness.

Pat yourself on the back for taking this journey.

15th September

To have a pet in your life brings you such love and joy.

Along with this comes responsibility. They need taking care of, nurturing, feeding, walking and much of your time and energy. They rely on you.

A pet such as a dog would not enjoy being left alone all day, or shut away for hours at a time. It wouldn't be fair. Even though they will be happy to see you and wag their tails, it is not much of a life for them.

Treat animals with love and respect and you will get that back in life. To be unkind to animals will bring unkindness to yourself.

16th September

Do you take responsibility for your own life? Or do you let others take the responsibility from you, make decisions for you, sort out your problems and challenges? In other words do you choreograph your own life?

Are you constantly blaming others for how your life is turning out?

17th September

When you are ill, do you acknowledge this yourself?

If people, as in family around you, ignore the fact that you are ill, then this will annoy you. But why should they if you are not acknowledging you are unwell yourself.

Stop; get off the treadmill and rest until you are healed.

18th September

When you need nurturing, do you acknowledge this?

Spend today looking after yourself, nurture yourself in the best way you can. Don't wait until you are ill.

One thing is for sure, if you don't nurture yourself, then no one else will.

Make sure you eat well, take time for rest and relaxation, and take some nurturing treatments or practices.

19th September

This is a time of year to appreciate the abundance of nature – harvest berries, mushrooms, seeds etc. – use what nature provides for us.

If you have space in your garden then perhaps plan a vegetable plot. Use any space for growing potatoes, vegetables and herbs. You can grow beautiful tomatoes, herbs, greens etc. even in pots on a small balcony or window ledge.

There is nothing more satisfying than growing your own food, harvesting your 'crop' and then eating your own nurtured and nutritious fresh food.

20th September

Observe the changes out in nature. See how the leaves are changing colour. How magical is this? How beautiful to be in touch with nature, Earth and the changing seasons.

See the berries in abundance – why not go out and pick some blackberries to use now or to freeze and use later. Also mushrooms grow in certain places and field mushrooms are delicious when picked fresh. Make a point of taking further studies and perhaps go on a foraging day with an expert, it is fun and you learn about edible mushrooms and fungi and the ones not to eat.

See the beauty – how green nature looks before the season changes. Try and spend as much time outside while you still can, before the cold months set it.

Give your thanks to Mother Nature and the abundance of Earth.

21st September

Today is Autumn Equinox. Day and night are equal in length. Now the nights will start to draw out, the light starts to fade. This is a most beautiful time of year – a time of magic and change.

Nature is changing and preparing for Winter. Be in tune with this and be prepared for Winter yourself.

22nd September

Winter is not a time to dread but a beautiful season to embrace. We spend more time indoors so this is a lovely time for relaxing more. Time for reading, writing or being more creative. Time to be still more and go inward.

Perhaps this winter is the one to search your inner world – to go into the deep You, the Deep Feminine.

This will help to balance your Male and Female energies, your Sun and Moon, so you can reach equilibrium.

23rd September

There is no better way to spend an enjoyable evening than with friends, sharing food. The food doesn't have to be lavish and break your bank balance. It is more the occasion of being together and being asked to share that is a joy.

It is comforting to know that someone is thinking of you and it is lovely for someone else to prepare and cook food for you.

Celebrate and acknowledge and appreciate where your food has come from. If you are eating meat then give your thanks to the animal and bless your food.

24th September

When you plant a seed of a vegetable, flower or tree in the Earth, the roots go down, into Mother Earth. Then the shoot will grow towards the light. See this likened to your own personal spiritual journey.

Earth your energies, ground your wounds, go into your dark inner world, clear your lower chakras. Without strong roots you will be blown off course from your path.

Once you are truly grounded and have connected with Mother Earth you will also grow towards the Light – have times of equilibrium and enlightenment.

25th September

Once you start to clear your lower chakras, your upper chakras will automatically start to cleanse especially if you practice regular meditation.

The upper chakras from the heart, throat, brow and crown are known as the spiritual centres. Although each chakra is a spiritual centre, the upper chakras especially link with Spirit energy, that is the Great Divine.

Take a meditation practice linking your upper chakras with the Great Divine i.e. focus on the heart, expand your energy out and link in.

26th September

The most beautiful gift of life is Compassion. This gift of Compassion is a gift to You and others.

Compassion is there within you, but in modern society, it can be well hidden and we have forgotten how to be compassionate and certainly how to receive compassion.

Place something around your home that will remind you of compassion, maybe a Buddha picture or ornament, red roses, pink candles, the 'Om Mane Padme Hum' Buddhist chant of compassion – whatever it is that links you to your heart chakra – the place of compassion.

27th September

If you feel that life is hectic, chaotic and so full that you feel you may burst with the overwhelming thought of your duties and tasks ahead today, then it is time to make changes and slow down, otherwise the stress will get to you, you may get ill and then you will be unable to do anything at all.

By slowing down to centre yourself for a few minutes every day, connect to the Self and connect to the Universe, you will achieve much more.

28th September

Practice centring yourself by creating a sacred space in a still, quiet environment. This can be in your home, office, work place, out in nature, anywhere.

Take a few minutes to get comfortable and relax your body. Breathe up energy from Mother Earth into your heart by imagining the energy coming up from the ground into your feet, up your legs, into the base of your body, up your lower body and into your heart energy centre. Take your time and spend several minutes on this.

Now take your focus above your head – either just above your Crown or much higher in to the cosmos. Breathe in energy from The Great Divine by imagining energy or a light coming down into your Crown, in to your head, down your neck, into your upper body and to your heart.

Now keep the focus at your Centre – your Heart and see the energy expanding.

Be at Peace, in Love and Compassion.

To be centred is such a wonderful place to be.

29th September

There will be times when the only way to connect is to go out in nature – take a walk but notice nature around you, notice the trees – the standing ones and see how still they are from the trunk down. Notice the beautiful colours of nature. Notice wildlife – the birds, rabbits, foxes, butterflies or whatever nature presents to you.

30th September

If a great song that moves you comes on the radio, then stop and listen. Let the song move you literally by letting your physical body move, let your emotions move freely – cry, laugh, shout, sing! Allow your body to naturally go where it wants to go which means don't try and think or choreograph a dance or movement, just move with the music and let it flow.

Music is so healing. Just know that no one is watching or judging you, lose your inhibitions, let go and be free, just as a child would.

You could be quite still with your feet but sway to the music or you could be jumping around crazily, whatever you fancy, let your inner child play.

Chapter Ten

1st October

A new month begins which takes us a little further into Autumn. How beautiful nature is at this time of year.

The leaves are starting to change colour. Some trees have incredible and most beautiful coloured leaves of reds and golds. These colours are heart-warming and it is a lovely time to go out with your camera, or paintbrush and capture the beauty. Colours have different effects on us and we all have different feelings towards colours. See what colours you wear, have in your home. Get a feel for these colours in your body.

Autumn reds and golds tend to be very warming colours.

2nd October

Today was the birth date of Ghandi. Ghandi left his mark on Earth which has benefited generations after him. His particular teaching was 'Ahimsa' which means non-violence. He proved that you can make your valid point and put it across in such a way that would not harm any living creature. His talks, marches and rallies were based on not bringing any forced action or violence.

He achieved peace and has influenced millions.

3rd October

Today have some thought as to what mark you would leave if you died.

What legacy would you leave behind? How do you think people would remember you?

Are you leaving behind anything that you are proud of, or not proud of?

4th October

If you only had a few weeks to live, is there anything in particular you would like to do, for instance make up with someone you fell out with, visit a country such as India or visit a sacred site such as Machu Pichu in Peru?

Why not do these things anyway?

5th October

Lack of affection in a person's life is a terrible lack of love and nurturing. This lack of affection can often lead to low self-worth and low fulfilment in life. This can then lead to depression and a mental illness.

As human beings, we need love and affection from birth to death and it is so sad if this is missing in a person's life.

6th October

To spend time with like-minded people is to pass away time with fulfilment and you will be left feeling full, optimistic and positive.

To spend time with someone who is not on your wavelength means the energy exchange is imbalanced which means maybe you are giving away too much of your energy. This will leave you feeling tired, drained, unfulfilled and out of balance.

When you take a path of healing and self-development, sometimes it is not easy and at times frustrating when you are in the company of people who have not taken this path, and are full of wounds and illnesses. But this is where Compassion comes in, you have compassion for where they are in life and each one of us has free will to walk our own paths.

7th October

If a Tyrant appears in your life and is goading you in to an argument or unpleasant discussion then try to be calm, but firm. If they then start shouting at you and throw insults, then also have firmness in your voice but still be calm.

If you start throwing insults at them, then the situation is hopeless.

8th October

If someone has a go at you in an unreasonable manner then often it is their issues that have arisen.

Often they sub-consciously want what you have in terms of kindness and love. They can rant at you because what they really want is what you have, and inside this infuriates them which make them angry. So they then take it out on someone else which is you.

They want your light but this is not something that can be taken, this comes from self-development, healing, discipline and hard work.

9th October

Does this mean that you can only spend time with like-minded spiritual people? Of course not but it does mean that you will be challenged and Tyrants will appear in your life.

These types of relationships will give you more grief, will be like a rollercoaster, and will be most challenging to you.

10th October

A balanced relationship with a friend or romantic partner will provide you with an equal exchange of energy.

An imbalanced relationship will leave one of you feeling tired and drained.

You will know when a relationship is no longer serving you as you will play scenarios in your mind of irritating scenes for instance you will fester and internalize things that are getting to you.

This will be draining your energy. Perhaps this relationship is no longer serving you.

11th October

Can you be honest and tell someone how you are feeling? What is their reaction when voicing your honesty? Not many people can take any form of criticism without getting offended so be careful of how you say things.

Turn this around and think how you would react and if people can be open about their feelings.

An evolved Soul will be able to openly discuss feelings without getting offended and personal. A wounded Soul will be most offended and will project their hurt onto you.

12th October

How about being honest with yourself?

Be honest with yourself by honouring your true feelings. Do not deny your inner voice of truth by ignoring it?

Within you is a wise person that can counsel and guide you with decisions such as a geographical location, a relationship, a specific career, a certain lifestyle.

So take note of your own feelings and do not deny them.

13th October

Today contemplate on acceptance. Once you have accepted a situation such as a relationship break-up or divorce, a death of a loved one, you can begin the letting go process. This will take much time.

This doesn't mean accepting your lot in life, being miserable and putting up with bullshit, this means accepting what has happened, has happened for a reason and The Great Divine is working with you and not against you.

14th October

Accepting often means adapting to changes in life. Go with change with positive energy and outlook.

If you resist change, life will be difficult, negative and you will feel like you are struggling and not progressing.

Feel the excitement that change brings, be open and you will go along with ease, fun, meet new people for instance.

15th October

Letting go of situations like a divorce, bereavement, a past trauma or wound will make you feel like a new person. Your suffering and struggling will be released, your emotional pain will go and you will feel healthy in your body, mind and spirit.

To hold on and suppress the past creates blocked energy in your body which can manifest into a disease or an illness.

Let Go and

Be Free.

16th October

To help you ground old energy spend today connecting with nature – outdoors, among trees, plants and wildlife.

Mother Earth will heal you and help you release your blocked energy so get really connected with her today.

Spend time in your favourite 'sit-spot', tune in with the abundance of the Plant World, feeling connected.

Look for signs such as movement, birds, sounds and feel energized.

17th October

When something happens in life that creates a big change then trust that this is a challenge to help you evolve on many levels.

When you let go of old energy and past wounds then try to release any fears that you hold for the future. Each day, take a step forward and go with the flow and ebb of life.

Move forward fearlessly with strength and courage.

Trust the Universe.

18th October

When you are in a calm and balanced state with your mind quiet, your intuition guides you, rather than your ego.

Learn to identify your intuitive and true voice from your heart rather than your false ego from your head.

Learn to trust your Intuition for this is your own power, your inner wisdom.

Meditation will quieten your logical mind and awaken your intuitive mind.

19th October

Sometimes life can really get on top of you. You are tired, even exhausted. You are so irritable you feel almost murderous.

Time to take a break, get away from your normal routine, people, work.

A vacation would be ideal if it is viable. It does not have to be a flash five-star holiday, just a change of scene to get away from routines and stress. This will renew your energy.

20th October

Often it is too easy to focus on what is negative around you, all the bad bits, rather than give thanks and count your blessings. We often take for granted such things as:

Being grateful for life itself
Good health and able body
A roof over our heads
Warmth and food
Family and friends

21st October

Check your area to see if you have a sacred site such as a stone circle, ancient monument, a sacred place nearby.

These places are built on energy lines known as Ley Lines and have special energy and power.

Make plans to visit such a place and when you visit these places, treat them with respect for they are ancient sites used for ceremony. Ceremonies such as honouring the equinoxes and solstices would have taken place here and folk for miles around would have gathered. They would have also celebrated rites of passage such as birth, puberty, entering adulthood and becoming an elder in the village as well as marriages and another rite of passage which is death.

Feel the energy by touching the stones and getting a real feel for the place. Visit alone or with like-minded people who will not want to rush.

Spend time connecting to these special places.

22nd October

Folklore suggests that these sacred sites are inhabited by little Earthlings such as faeries, elves and leprechauns – why not close your eyes whilst at a sacred site, be a child, be in trust and innocence and let your imagination run wild and free – see these little earth beings. Connect with then – they are little beings of Mother Earth. Their Spirit is uplifting, joyful and fun and can be also mischievous and cheeky.

23rd October

Maybe you have a place of pilgrimage in mind such as Tibet, India, Peru or to a place such as an ancient temple like Ankor Wat in Cambodia.

Often there are places much closer to home for you to make your pilgrimage to. You are in your environment and geographical location for a reason and it is part of your spiritual journey to discover this.

Often Travellers will seek and wander the world searching only what is after all inside themselves.

24th October

Travellers and Spiritual Aspirants are looking for the same thing. They are trying to 'find themselves' which means liberation of the Soul, detachment from the Ego-Self.

That will bring relief from suffering, happiness and to live in a state of equilibrium, with one foot in the Spirit Energies and one foot in the Earth Energies.

25th October

Detachment of the Ego-Self is being in connection with the Soul.

You will still have consciousness of the fact you are still you in your physical body. But your mind will be free from baggage of the past, you will not have extreme emotions of lust, anger, jealously, fear and hatred. You will live simply and be content.

You will continue with your spiritual practice of meditating and studying and you will incorporate what you have learnt into daily life.

You will experience pure meditation which will continue to bring you into this peaceful place.

26th October

Your spiritual practice is a continuous journey and the further you walk your path then you will have moments of feeling really free and liberated.

Then these moments can be sustained for longer periods of time and then you can live your life in a place of balance and happiness.

You can now walk in your own power.

You will emanate love, compassion and peace.

27th October

Every now and then a Tyrant will still appear in your life to 'test' you. A person who you will find challenging and who will push your buttons. But if they make you angry then don't hold onto this anger – just let it go. If this Tyrant is judgemental, critical, rants, opinionated – don't let it bother you, let it go over your head rather than holding the energy in your body.

You have learnt to not take on any energy that is harmful to you, you let it wash over you. This is good karma.

28th October

Once you understand the concept of the Ego and working at a Soul level, you will be guided and led in life by your intuition – the truth. This is rather that being led by the Ego – the distorted truth.

The true Self is the Soul. Your mind exists through the Soul when you have detached yourself from your Ego. You can then gain access to the higher truths – the inner wisdom that we all have locked away inside us.

29th October

Make a list of the Tyrants who have appeared in your life and what they teach you about yourself, for example:

Friend called Paul who showers me with gifts and is really nice to me but then expects so much back. What I can learn is not to take gifts from someone like Paul who then makes me feel beholden to him.

Father called William who constantly rants about his opinionated views. What I can learn is to not offload my crap on to someone who doesn't deserve to have an ear bashing from me.

Mother-in-law Hilda who talks and talks at you rather than with you and never listens to anything I want to say. It is all about her all the time and she drives me mad. What I can learn is to listen and hold the space when others are talking and to detach myself from their negative energies. Also not to talk *at* people which makes them feel disengaged and irritable but to have conversation *with* people.

And so on.

30th October

If you have an affinity to a particular animal, the chances are this animal can guide and teach you something. It is really a pleasure to connect with your own Power Animal, your ally, your animal friend and most useful.

To connect with your Power Animal, take the following practice. Prepare yourself and your space around you for Meditation. Close your eyes and allow a few minutes to relax and prepare. In your mind have the intention of connecting with your Power Animal.

Visualize yourself out in nature – out in a landscape, whatever comes to your mind.

Be still in this environment and invite your ally, your Power Animal to join you. Wait and be patient. Trust what you see. Connect with the energy of this animal. How does this feel? Ask what your Power Animal can teach you, what guidance it brings.

31st October

Today is the celebration of Samhain which means the beginning of Winter, the darkest time of year, when the skies are cold and dark. Honour this as a period of rest, regeneration and renewal.

In modern times today is known as Halloween and this is a special time when the veil between the two Worlds is said to be at its thinnest. A time of year to honour our Ancestors and lost loved ones which is known as the 'Festival of the Dead'.

Chapter Eleven

1st November

Try to not dread the winter months for fear of being cold, dark and depressed. See this as a time for slowing down and withdrawing. A time for resting more indoors, warming yourself by the fire and being cosy.

2nd November

Some adjustment will be needed – time to swap the wardrobe round – get out the winter woollies, hats, scarves and gloves in preparation for colder weather.

If you have an open fire or log burner, go out into the forest and collect wood, particularly kindling.

Note how rewarding it is to gather your own wood, rather than paying to have it delivered.

Light a fire in the evening or a candle and simply be, watching the flames.

Thank Grandfather Fire for the warmth and energy.

3rd November

Once you acknowledge and accept this change of season rather than begrudge it, you can let go of attachments to the summer and autumn which will enable you to move on in many aspects of your life.

This will be empowering, and you will feel brighter.

4th November

If you get certain days that trigger off dark moods, think of a way to brighten up your day.

What works for you? Try a good brisk walk and on a crisp November day this can be beautiful, uplifting, healing and nurturing.

If you get dark days which lead to depression then really put some energy in to shifting this blocked energy from your mind and from your body.

5th November

This time of year is not a time to do too much, to fill your diary, to have a full-on social life. Be in tune – drift, dream, have visions.

This is a powerful time to meditate and the more you allow your energy to settle after summer and autumn and enter into the winter months, the more inward you will go and this is a healthy natural place to be for this time of year. Spend more time being still, practicing meditation and being peaceful.

6th November

The sun cannot shine every day.

If it rains and pours on some days, then brighten your day by lighting your internal flame:

Sit quietly – create your sacred space around you.

Breathe – focus on your breath.

Relax – take your time and let your whole body relax.

See a light being switched on inside you. This light is your Soul and by being still and focused, you are connecting at a Soul level. See this light getting brighter and brighter within.

7th November

Your thoughts can be changed. Often your thoughts are self-destructive and self-critical which is very draining as the energy that follows these thoughts will produce negative feelings and emotions.

If you don't have these negative thoughts then you won't have these negative feelings.

Change the thought and the feeling will change.

8th November

If you are continuously re-living your past, then you will not be able to leave this behind and move on.

Often re-living your past will be painful and this no longer serves us. It is often comfortable to be stuck in this pain because that is the habit that you know.

Release this energy and get out of your rut.

You will be amazed how refreshing this is.

9th November

The choice is yours – be free, be liberated from suffering.

Or stay stuck in the past, be stuck in old habits, routines and patterns.

What feels best?

The choice is yours as you have Free Will.

10th November

If you are constantly telling yourself 'I am not good enough' then that is what you will believe.

You will block joy, happiness and self-love.

Tell yourself 'I am good enough and I am worthy'.

Bring joy, happiness and self-love into your life.

11th November

Today is the 11th day of the 11th month and is a day for meditation and spiritual growth.

Spend some time today in peace and quiet, and in contemplation.

Reflect on what your main challenge is in life right now for you and what is reflected back to you from other people in your life. This means looking at the Tyrants and what they can teach you about yourself as a mirror.

12th November

Today, spare at least a thought to someone who you could send out love, nurturing and healing to.

If you can do a nice deed for someone such as visit an elderly person or someone who is in need of company. Is there someone you could offer a lift to if they don't drive or have a car?

Call an old friend to see how they are.

13th November

It's never too late to be, what you could have been.

Get in contact with your fire energy and do those things in life that you have always wanted to do.

14th November

If you are constantly feeling lethargic and tired, then perhaps some changes could be made in your lifestyle.

Firstly assess your diet and your intake of alcohol, caffeine, heavy foods such as red meat, starchy carbohydrates. See what changes you can make such as eat more fish and have some days with no meat.

Take some exercise each day – what could be better for you than a 20-minute walk in the fresh air?

Maximize your wellbeing and revitalize your life.

15th November

The problems that confront us in life generally are created by man, whether they are violent conflicts, wars, destruction of the planet.

If only countries where there is war would come together and resolve their problems.

As a human race we must cultivate a universal responsibility to each other and towards saving the Planet.

16th November

The 'old ways' which have never actually been lost but have been suppressed over the years will be prevalent in this century. The old ways are ancient values which mean honouring and respecting every other human being.

It also means honouring and respecting Mother Earth. Appreciating what she provides us with in terms of life, food, wood to keep warm and the beauty of nature itself.

Communities will re-form and the weak, sick and elderly will be better looked after. Life will be back to simple and being content, free from desires. People will be living in their centre, their heart rather than the crazy energy of their heads.

17th November

Guilt, fear, criticism (of self as well as others), hatred, resentment are all energies that if stored in our body will cause all sorts of problems.

Guilt is a waste of energy. Fear will cause stress, anxiety and can lead to aggression.

Criticising yourself will restrict you in many ways and will give yourself grief and misery.

Hatred is a bitter energy. Resentment will get you nowhere. You cannot change the past.

18th November

You may not be able to change your past, but you can choreograph your own life and your future using your free will, strength and courage. You can set a future for yourself that fulfils your own desires, ambitions, needs and wishes.

19th November

The Universe will support you in your choice of thoughts. This means that if you feel helpless, you are a victim, then that is what you are.

If you have continual resentment, then that is what you are.

If you are liberated from suffering, have peaceful thoughts, then that is what you are.

If your thoughts are positive and you have an uplifting bright outlook, then that is what you are.

20th November

It's all very well saying be bright, positive, don't be resentful, negative, sad. What if you have a past of abuse, neglect, abandonment?

It would take a very positive person to heal the wounds of the past without the help of a Therapist or Practitioner. The wounds can be buried deep inside.

It will take many sessions of hard work which will need strength and courage and the willingness to forgive. Forgiveness of other people involved and just as importantly forgiveness of the Self.

21st November

If you go through life continuously blaming others then you will not evolve as you are not taking responsibility for your own actions.

If you go through life continuously focusing on your ill-health and diseases of the body, then it will be very difficult to be healed. Best to look at the underlying causes rather than keep suppressing the symptoms with medication that often have side-effects which trigger off more disease in the body.

22nd November

When in a dispute and disagreement with someone and you are adamant that you are right, why not try having compassion and love for the other person and try to see things from their perspective and point of view.

It is frustrating when you are fighting your corner and stating your point of view. Try fighting from the other corner. See how that feels.

23rd November

If on the other hand, a person never sees your point of view and they always think they are right then energies are not in balance between you.

If this person always questions what you say, and tries to correct you continuously then that is disempowering for you.

If this person is childish, stubborn and rants and raves at you, then it is likely that they are a Tyrant in your life. They are in your life to challenge you so you can evolve.

24th November

This type of Tyrant is known as a Sociopath.

A Sociopath has the following traits:

Superficial charm
Manipulative
Lack of remorse, shame or guilt
Exaggerates or lies
Outbursts of anger
Cannot perceive anything is wrong with them
Control freaks
Nothing is ever their fault
Always put blame elsewhere
Incapable of real love
Only know needy love

25th November

A Psychopath has all the traits of a Sociopath but have rather disturbing extra ones.

A Psychopath has a lack of conscious and is completely self-serving. If they hurt others whether human or from the animal world, they will show no remorse or guilt.

They do not feel for others but are very clever at appearing to be very normal.

Psychopaths are often well-educated and their crimes tend to be well-organized.

26th November

If you are in a bad relationship that is continuously giving you grief and stress then perhaps it is time to do some work in this area.

Counselling for couples is a very good start.

If you don't learn from relationships, you will continuously drift from one to another, making the same mistakes, picking the same sort of person and be stuck in a wheel of repeated patterns.

This applies to friendships as well as partners.

27th November

Spend today just 'being'. No chores or tasks that can wait until another day.

Just 'Be'

Do nothing

Say nothing

Think of nothing

28th November

Today meditate on the word 'Hope'.

Be hopeful and have confidence in the future.

Life is a gift and it is better to live with light and optimism rather than dark pessimism.

29th November

Today you are invited to connect with your Guardian Angel.

Prepare your space for meditation, close your eyes, focus on your breath and give yourself several minutes to settle, allowing the whole body to feel relaxed and free from tension.

Now take your focus to your heart and open your heart energy centre by visualizing a beautiful pink flower with the petals open. Each time you exhale feel the energy around your heart getting stronger.

Invite your Guardian Angel to come close to you so you can feel the energy. If you need guidance, healing or love then ask your Angel for this.

You may visualize an Angel, you may see Angelic colours which are usually purple, green, gold or white. You may feel a beautiful energy around your heart. You may feel warmth or even cool energy. There is no right or wrong.

Give yourself several minutes and enjoy being in this wonderful space.

When you feel you are done, give your thanks to the Angel Realm, and ground yourself and drink some water.

30th November

Pets have Souls also.

Our pets are precious to us, they give us unconditional love, healing, warmth and companionship.

Like yourself, your pet is a spirit in a physical body.

Their level of consciousness is of a different vibration to humans but they still have an element of intelligence and communication can take place at a certain level.

Animals tend to live completely in the present and are totally instinctive creatures in tune with nature and the seasons. They are very knowing and you will hear of lovely stories where pets love and comfort their owners, give them healing and know when something is not right as they are psychic. Their senses are heightened and they really are the most wonderful companions.

Chapter Twelve

1st December

The beginning of the last month of the year where another door begins to shut and a new one opens.

This is a good time for reflection of the last eleven months and to think of any goals or achievements that are unmet that could still be met.

You still have one month before the wheel turns round again – a new year will begin – fresh energy will come into your life.

2nd December

With the Festive Season fast approaching this can be a difficult time for those who have lost loved ones.

Traditionally Christmas is a time of family gathering – we like to present to the outer world a family of peace and harmony which often is not reality. When a loved one has passed to Spirit, it is times like this when spells of grief can return.

Try to think of happy memories with your lost loved one.

When you get feelings of sadness, let the emotion run through you, let the tears flow. Allow yourself to have these moments, it is normal.

Tomorrow will be another day.

3rd December

When you have lost a loved one, their physical body is no more. But their Spirit is immortal and lives through the Soul.

Often you will feel their spirit close to you. They may come to you in dreams. You may feel their presence when you are still and relaxed and your mind is not active.

Do not be fearful, welcome the energy and it can provide you with love and reassurance when you need it.

You will feel supported and guided if you open your heart.

4th December

Death is a rite of passage that we all journey towards. It is true that life is short so make the most out of each and every day.

Be happy and positive and you will enjoy life and be a pleasure to be around.

5th December

It is true that we are sent signs from the spirit world. A common one is a white feather which often appears out of nowhere when you least expect it.

Perhaps a bird or butterfly flies close to you. A bird of prey may fly above you when you need to feel and see this energy.

Maybe you were thinking of a song and then it is played on the radio or you hear a tune that resonates with your memory.

Maybe you are having experiences of synchronicity which are a bit like experiences of coincidence but this is different and more powerful.

6th December

Just spare a thought for all the paper that is used from the trees to provide most households in your country with Christmas cards.

Think of the monstrous volumes and see where you can cut down on cards.

7th December

Today, spend some time on reflecting and prayer.

Pray for unity and peace among all people.

The energy from your thoughts and prayers will be sent out to the Universe – the energy of unity and peace.

8th December

We can do without religion in life, but not without spirituality.

Religion is full of dogma and beliefs and is often placing

women in disempowerment.

Spirituality is love and compassion, unity and peace amongst all people, for you are God.

9th December

What would be the point of giving away your money to charity if you have not enough food and shelter for yourself and your family?

What would be the point in spending your Christmas looking after a charitable cause if your own family suffer with your absence?

Maybe that is their lesson but there is a lot of truth in the saying 'charity begins at home'. You can't go giving away all your energy and money if your family needs feeding first.

There is a difference to sharing and giving what you don't have.

10th December

But today, on the other hand remember that Christmas is a time of sharing and a time of open hearts that think of others.

Best to get this into perspective and balance.

11th December

If doing any charity work or donating a gift of money, give from the right place which is your heart.

If you are doing it to make you feel better, less guilty, then the intention is not right.

Give because you want to without expecting anything in return.

Give from your heart.

12th December

Don't have high expectations of Christmas, and then you won't be disappointed.

Just relax, enjoy the build-up, without expecting too much from it.

You may be pleasantly surprised instead.

13th December

Try not to put too much pressure on yourself at this time of year.

It makes sense to not buy expensive presents if funds are not there. Another suggestion is to agree to give token gifts or agree to not exchange gifts at all.

You will probably be pleasantly surprised at their relief.

14th December

To spend, spend, spend and get caught up in commercial consumerism will bring misery when your bank statement comes through in January.

It would feel way better to start next year with a healthy bank balance than to start the year with credit card bills and debts.

Christmas will pass quickly, so enjoy this time of year but avoid getting caught up in the spending trap.

15th December

Why not spend every day like Christmas Day – a day of joy and celebration of life.

16th December

Try and see beyond the glitz, the bright lights, tinsel.

Try and see the warmth in people's hearts – have compassion for all beings.

If a person appears to be nasty, angry and grumpy – have compassion for an unhappy, wounded Soul.

17th December

Try to give yourself a few minutes every day for quiet time.

No thinking about the past, no thinking about the future. Just being.

Have a gentle stretch – stretch your arms, your legs, and your whole body.

Meditate for ten minutes just focusing on your breath, with every out breath – let go of tension and stress – particularly around your neck and shoulders.

You will benefit from this when times get hectic and stressful.

18th December

Regular meditation will help to de-clutter your mind, useless baggage will be cleared. Ego hangs on to past wounds.

Just imagine how that would feel, imagine what it would be like to have a calm mind, a healthy body, a calm nervous system, clear spirit.

By practicing regular meditation you can experience it, feel it.

19th December

When you are meditating your mind becomes still, your body is still.

This is a powerful place of healing.

It is essential to give yourself time for this on a regular basis – give it priority and then you will automatically include this into your daily routine.

20th December

Today, spend some time connecting to your inner world. Your inner world is your Deep Feminine, your Dark.

Prepare the space around you for meditation. Prepare yourself by making sure you are warm and comfortable and close your eyes. Let your breath settle and allow your whole body to feel relaxed which may take several minutes.

Take your awareness inside your physical body.

Take your awareness deeper with every exhale.

Don't try to see anything, just be in the Dark within. Let go of tension and fear.

This is a place of beauty and peace.

Tonight would be a good night to stay up for a few extra hours or even all night and really be with the dark, bring in the Winter Solstice morning.

21st December

Today is Winter Solstice – the shortest day of the year in terms of light and the longest night.

This is the end of a cycle. Give yourself time to reflect over the last six months to the Summer Solstice on 21st June. Reflect on your challenges and learn from them.

Leave behind old energy and emotions – don't carry these on into the fresh New Year.

Go inwards, into the Dark, have a long night's sleep.

22nd December

Remind yourself that this dark place that you can get in touch with is your inner world and is not a place of depression and dark in the negative sense. It is a place of the utmost peace and beauty.

Once you have really connected with this place, you will want to keep finding it as it makes you feel so calm and more able to cope with life and its ups and downs.

23rd December

Have a think about the word 'Balance'. To live life in balance is to be happy, healthy and in equilibrium. This is balance of your material world of money and career with your spiritual world of self-development, healing and being an aspirant.

Balance of your inner Male and Female energies will put you in a place of harmony.

Balance of spending time alone so you can evolve and then spending time with family and friends for companionship without making this a permanent distraction from your spiritual path.

Balance of your own needs and giving your time and energy to your family without totally draining yourself.

A Good balance of splitting your time between work and rest and play time.

With Christmas upon you a balance of eating and drinking and not overdoing it as we tend to do.

24th December

Once all your chores are done take some time to relax and recharge your batteries by practicing a Christmas Angel Healing Meditation. Prepare your space for meditation. Prepare yourself by getting yourself warm and comfortable. Close your eyes and allow your whole body to relax.

Take your awareness to your heart area and when you breathe in invite Christmas Healing Angels in. Take your time and stay focused. You may start to have feelings of love, warmth and elation. You may see visions of Angels with colours of whites, purples and golds especially. Ask for what you need which could be 'Please send me Healing, Love and Peace in my heart'.

Be patient, be open and enjoy this wonderful Christmas Angelic Healing Meditation.

When you feel done, as always give your thanks and then take your time to bring your awareness back and ground yourself by seeing roots going from your feet into Mother Earth and opening your eyes in your own time.

25th December

Today is the celebration of the birth of a very powerful Healer – Jesus.

Jesus was a selfless man, who spoke words of wisdom. He was detached from his ego and his mind was led by his intuition.

He was a pure channel of healing energy from Spirit who

emanated love, peace and compassion.

26th December

It is said that Jesus works as an Ascended master from the Spirit World to help and guide humans who are working with the right intention from the heart with love, peace and compassion – in the Light.

He will appear during powerful healing sessions to these Channellers of Light who are working in pure intention.

He also appears during the passing of a person over to the Spirit World to heal the Soul over during death.

27th December

If you are a Dualist then you believe that there is an external God rather like in religions but if you are a non-dualist then you know that you are God, you have God within you.

As a non-dualist your power is within you and not given away to anything external from yourself.

28th December

The happiness of life is made up of minute fractions – the little soon-forgotten charities of a kiss, a smile, a kind look, a heartfelt compliment.

Happiness resides not in possessions and not in money, the feeling of happiness dwells in the soul.

29th December

Laughter is the best medicine.

This is so true so spend time with people that make you laugh or watch a funny movie or go and see a comedian.

Laughter shifts energy – it makes you feel good and releases endorphins.

30th December

The main points to focus on to help you on your spiritual quest are:

Moving energy in the form of physical movement which can be in the form of Yoga Postures, Tai Chi or something where you are focusing on energy rather than just getting a physical sweaty workout to feed the ego.

To practice forms of breathing techniques. To focus on the breath, to learn to breathe using full capacity of the lungs.

To practice meditation – trying the various types of techniques such as focusing on the breath, using visualizations, working with sound – musical instruments, mantras – sacred sounds, chanting and finding a technique that works for you.

Work on healing your wounds, peel off the layers that have built up over the years developing patterns, holding on to the past, learn to let go. Learn from your challenges and lessons in life.

Be free, at peace, happy and healthy.

31st December

Close doors from the past and open new doors into the future. Go forth into the New Year with fresh energy, with courage

Don't focus on the closed doors behind you, but on the open doors in front of you.

Have a healthy and happy New Year!

X

Useful contacts

Michelle's website: www.purplebuddha.co.uk

Michelle's Books – 'Your Quest for a Spiritual Life', 'Your Quest for Spiritual Knowledge'. Meditation CD – Your Quest for Peace, Healing & Balance, all available from Amazon.

Eagle's Wing College of Shamanic Medicine – www.shamanism.co.uk

The British Wheel of Yoga – www.bwy.org.uk

BOOKS

O is a symbol of the world, of oneness and unity. In different cultures it also means the "eye," symbolizing knowledge and insight. We aim to publish books that are accessible, constructive and that challenge accepted opinion, both that of academia and the "moral majority."

Our books are available in all good English language bookstores worldwide. If you don't see the book on the shelves ask the bookstore to order it for you, quoting the ISBN number and title. Alternatively you can order online (all major online retail sites carry our titles) or contact the distributor in the relevant country, listed on the copyright page.

See our website **www.o-books.net** for a full list of over 500 titles, growing by 100 a year.

And tune in to myspiritradio.com for our book review radio show, hosted by June-Elleni Laine, where you can listen to the authors discussing their books.